CW00547638

# BEING WITH
# BENNY

# ABOUT THE AUTHOR

 BOB ROSS BEGAN SAILING AT the age of ten in the P-class trainer at the Plimmerton Boating Club on the shores of Cook Strait, New Zealand; he progressed to the two-handed Z-class then three-handed Idle Along.

After working in Wellington and New Plymouth as a journalist, Ross moved to Australia in 1955, aged 24 and worked on newspapers as a general reporter: Launceston Examiner (Tasmania), Daily Telegraph (Sydney) and finally the Sun News-Pictorial (Melbourne) from 1959.

At the Sun-Pic, in his spare time, he started a general boating column and began covering sailing. He went sailing again, on 21ft restricted class open boats, Lightweight Sharpies, Finns and keelboats on Port Phillip Bay and offshore.

Through Finns he met Colin Ryrie, the 1964 Olympic representative and 1964-65 Australian Finn class champion, who recruited him to be first editor of Modern Boating magazine, founded by Ryrie and business partner Jules Feldman, as the next magazine to Modern Motor in their growing Modern Magazines chain in Sydney.

After six years, Ross resigned and went freelance to become yachting correspondent for the Sydney Morning Herald and to write books.

With Ken McLachlan, business partner and advertising manager, he founded Australian Sailing, Australia's first all-sailing magazine, in 1976. He sold the magazine to the Yaffa Publishing Group of leisure magazines in 1986, and remained as editor until 2003.

# BEING WITH
# BENNY

---

## INSIDE THE WORLD OF
## BEN LEXCEN

First published in 2018
Copyright 2018 © Bob Ross
All rights reserved

Published by Boatswain Books • boatswainbooks.uk

ISBN: 978-1-912724-01-7

Designed and produced by Robert Deaves

All rights reserved. No part of this publication may be repro-
duced, stored in a retrieval system or transmitted in any form
by any means, electronic, mechanical, photocopying, recording or otherwise without the prior written permission of the
publisher, the author and any other copyright holders.

# CONTENTS

# FOREWORD

by John Bertrand

I FIRST MET BEN (BOB MILLER then) at the 1972 Olympics in Kiel, the home of the Olympic sailing events. Ben was sailing in the Solings, me the Finn, representing our country.

Ben and his crew of Denis O'Neill and Ken Berkeley, made an unlikely trio. But they were fast; fast in a breeze. The only problem was in Kiel, although the winds were meant to be strong, they were light; enough to do your head in. Ben was both super talented, in fact a genius, but also temperamental; an explosive combination. They eventually finished 16th. I able to win the 'leather medal' – fourth.

I had recently graduated from the Massachusetts Institute of Technology in Boston with a Master of Science. That was good enough for Ben to approach me to work on his America's Cup challenger Southern Cross, with Alan Bond the syndicate head.

I had already competed in the 1970 America's Cup on Gretel II with Jim Hardy as the skipper and Sir Frank Packer the syndicate head. But meeting Ben was the start of a new world for me and my bride Rasa.

So how would I describe Ben? Well, he was the Leonardo da Vinci of Australia, absolutely brilliant, a total lateral thinker. He basically had no formal education, which in many ways released him from conventional thinking. And he was funny. He was a raconteur. He could talk on any subject from art to politics, to world events. He was a student of life. And he became the godfather of our first born, Lucas.

Living and working in Sydney on the America's Cup project was a new world for Rasa and me and Ben was that new world. He would often come around to our small rented apartment and stay; sometimes for weeks. Just bunk in.

I remember one day; Ben and I were down at Bondi beach; a windy turbulent day. Ben was intently watching the seagulls land and take off. He said to me: 'Look at those seagulls. They never make a crash landing. Their take-offs are perfect each time.' He then went on to say: 'Each trailing edge wing feather has to be connected to tiny little nerves, each finally connecting to their tiny brains. Their brains cannot be any larger than a pea. But to do what they do; their flight controls have to be more sophisticated than a military jet.'

That was Ben, constantly monitoring Mother Nature, totally absorbed in the wonderment of 'why'.

The winged keel was Ben's greatest design achievement. It came out of his constant search for improvement. It was a brilliant solution to creating a faster boat within the America's Cup rule. And typical of Ben, on day one when we first launched Australia II in Fremantle, before we even hoisted sails, he said to me: 'Ahh, I need to change the stern. We can do better.'

Ben Lexcen, yes, a national treasure.

**John Bertrand AO**
*April 2018*

# I

# BOB MILLER

B EN LEXCEN, BORN BOB MILLER, emerged from a fractured childhood with a passion for sailing boats which fuelled a self-taught journey into yacht design that ended with the Twelve Metre Australia II he designed for Alan Bond winning yachting's most elusive prize, the America's Cup.

The lack of formal education in a way worked for Lexcen. The open mind and a hunger for new ideas led to his exploration of the winged keel concept, which crossed his path from aeronautical engineering while he was researching the Australia II design. He had experimented with wings many years earlier on a variety of craft. In the early 1960s, his Moth and his 18ft skiffs Taipan and Venom had 'gates' – small wings on the rudder. He also tried a winged centreboard on the 18s.

The extraordinary Australia II, with its upside-down winged keel giving it the stability to carry a large sail area on a smaller hull form, was faster in the light winds off Newport and quicker to spin in pre-start manoeu-

America's Cup presentation 1983, from left: John Bertrand,
Ben Lexcen, Alan Bond / KAORU SOEHATA

vres. Although Australia II began the match with equipment failures in
the first two races, probably the result of Lexcen's pre-occupation with
saving weight and the crew stumbled at times, eventually the boat, calmly
skippered by John Bertrand, more than anything else won the America's
Cup for Alan Bond's Australian team in 1983, ending the New York Yacht
Club's 132-year tenure of the trophy, the oldest winning streak in sport.

More than 20 years on, an older element in the New York Yacht Club
still believed the Australians cheated with the winged keel. While Bond
and Australia II's skipper, John Bertrand, along with skipper of previous
Australian challengers Sir James Hardy had long before been admitted
to the America's Cup Hall of Fame, established in 1993, Lexcen made it
only in 2006.

Lexcen died on May 1, 1988, from a heart attack. Warren Jones, who
managed the Australia II syndicate for Alan Bond, at the memorial ceremony for Ben at St Andrew's Cathedral in Sydney, on May 5, 1988,
said in the eulogy: 'He was one of those unique people who possessed
characteristics that separated him from most of us. He was so humble
and yet so proud, so simple and yet so complex, so everything.

'He could be 40 characters in one day, from philosopher, to engineer,
to clown, almost changing by the hour, dependent on the circumstance
or mood; most important of all never disguising that he was fundamen-
tally a humble person who had no wish to hide where he came from and
what he was – no pretences whatever, just him.'

Jones, who was one of Lexcen's closest friends, in the eulogy spoke also of Ben's compassion for children, suggesting it stemmed from his own difficult and disrupted childhood. Ben's last creation was a skateboard with wings that carried extra stabilising wings for beginners. It won him an award at the international toy fair in Sydney the week before his death.

Women loved Lexcen and Lexcen loved them. Married twice, as a young man to Dorothy and later to the older Yvonne, who added much-needed stability to his disorderly lifestyle, he maintained a series of casual affairs. His friends were not surprised when at the funeral service, a lovely-looking woman dressed in black, with a big hat she could have worn to the races, glided into St Andrews after the service had started, down to the front, to sit among Ben's closest Sydney friends. 'Who's she?' they all thought. She sobbed loudly and the minute before the service was over, she glided out.

Ben married Yvonne, a 55-year-old divorcee with two children, in 1976. She was strong, patient, determined, generous, and compassionate. She put up with Ben's mood meltdowns, eccentricities and casual affairs; gave him the security of a good home in Sydney and was by his side through the dramas of the America's Cup campaigning. Lexcen's closest friend Carl Ryves, says: 'She was a lovely lady and Benny definitely liked her. My wife Alysoun and I were good friends with Yvonne and Ben; we used to go out together for dinner about every week.

Above: Ben and Yvonne enjoying
a day on the water aboard their
Lexcen-designed motor cruiser
Right: Yvonne Lexcen
LEXCEN FAMILY ARCHIVE

'She gave him all that security with a house over his head while he was off buying Ferraris and racing around a little bit. He probably lived five years longer having someone caring for him so much.'

Lexcen was loyal to his friends and forgiving to his enemies, although that forgiveness sometimes took many years. A falling-out with his partner Craig Whitworth in their sailmaking/yacht design business led to his surprising name change by deed poll from Bob Miller to Ben Lexcen early in 1977. But in later years, he never said a bad word about Craig.

Concern for his friends was not changed by the fame that came to him through the America's Cup win, although the pressures of the Cup campaign and the glad-handing aftermath sometimes necessarily distanced him from them.

Being with Benny was never boring; always entertaining, often hilarious, sometimes outrageous and occasionally sad. His visits to the offices of Australian Sailing magazine in Sydney used to bring the whole place to a standstill as we gathered to hear the latest anecdote; the latest idea to make boats go faster. He had a wonderful sense of humour and a zany perception of life in general.

Could he liven up a party? What about the time, at the Mexico Olympics in 1968, when he hired a mariachi band he'd heard playing quite badly at the bullfights, to play at the Australian party at the end of the Games and almost got them thrown out of the hotel?

He was exceptionally good sailor in every type of boat he took on from Flying Dutchman dinghies, to Soling keelboats, to ocean racers. He won selection in the Australian Olympic team for the 1972 Games as helmsman in the Soling class. Lifelong friend Carl Ryves, also an Olympian in the Flying Dutchman class, says: 'He was probably better than any of us, but he didn't have the temperament to put it all together. He was never satisfied, always thinking of new ideas, new fittings, new shapes, streamlining sail shapes, neat fittings.'

Sailing with him was a rewarding experience when things were going right. He was a clever tactician, wonderful technician and a good teacher. On a bad day, however, bad became worse. I remember one race, on a Half Tonner he designed that proved a total failure, when he rushed forward to help correct a crewing error. In untangling the spinnaker, his expensive new watch went over the side and he retired below, head in hands, and told us, 'You are the worst crew I have ever sailed with.'

Fast cars were a passion and suited his impatient nature. Traversing the Sydney Harbour Bridge with Benny in one of his favoured Ferraris usually involved seven lane changes.

Inanimate objects were often at risk in his presence. Shackles that could not be opened readily with the fingers were tossed overboard. A power drill that would not work could be hurled against a wall. A telephone handset flew out the window from the offices of the Lexcen & Lowe design team into the waters of Careening Cove one day. Benny did not like what he was hearing over it from Colin Beashel in Fremantle, preparing for the Bond team's unsuccessful attempt to defend the America's Cup in 1987.

He developed a passion for classical music, steadily and markedly from the days he used to play the harmonica under the shower at the home of a sailing family he adopted, the Ryves of Hunters Hill, wearing the only pair of pants that he owned at the time. He washed the drip-dry pants and shirt at the same time as the body, for economy of effort and a saving of water and then walked around in them until they were dry.

HE COULD HAVE been an artist. Carl Ryves remembers: 'When we were kids and he used to live at our place, he always had a sketch book under his arm and he could really draw well; people, anything.' Ben's drawings in later years, of cars, boats and their bits were reminiscent of those of Leonardo da Vinci. A keel design he drew freehand for Australia III in the 1987 America's Cup defence proved faster than its predecessor from the test tank.

He drew the lines of a successful 16ft skiff on the back of an afternoon newspaper in a pub. In casual conversation on yacht design with Sydney 18ft skiff builder and sailor Len Heffernan, to demonstrate the concept of what an ideal Quarter Tonner should be, he drew a datum line down the wall of Heffernan's shed and then the sections.

'A year or two later a chap came down to see me, looked at the drawing on the wall and said, 'What's that there?'' Heffernan recalled.

'I said, 'Bobby Miller drew what he thought a Quarter Tonner should be like.''

'If I take this sheet of fibro can I replace it?'

'I said, 'Yeah, help yourself'. I believe he built a boat off it, from the free-hand drawing. Bob was a very good drawer.'

BACK IN 1971 I became publicist for the embryo yacht design arm of Miller & Whitworth, sailmakers and yacht chandlers and admitted to the magical circle of Bob Miller's friends. At 34 he already had firm achievements behind him. One of his lightweight three-handed boats, Taipan, had overturned convention in the 18ft skiff class in 1960 and its successor, Venom, won the J.J.Giltinan international championship in 1961. Crewing for his business partner Craig Whitworth, he had won three Australian championships and one Interdominion (Australia/New Zealand) championship in the Flying Dutchman class.

The 18-footers came while Ben was working in Brisbane for a time; encouraged by Norm Wright, to start a sailmaking loft over the Wright family's boatshed. Norm, successful in the powerful 18s of that time, with crews of four and five and much more sail area than Taipan and the following boat Venom, encouraged Ben's lateral thought processes.

'Norm Wright was a good bloke for me because he would never put the kibosh on any idea I had, no matter how mad it was, he would always encourage me. And it was a great thing for me. Most people, if I get a mad idea tend to throw cold water on them and I get mad ideas every day. And if I don't have mad ideas and do some of them I go stale; I get sick to death of being alive.'

Bob Miller had also designed the trapeze-powered Contender which, sailed by Whitworth, won the International Yacht Racing Union's trials to select a new single-handed dinghy class in 1968.

He was about to design a string of successful offshore yachts, like Ginkgo and Apollo II, which were to sail for Australia in the Admiral's Cup of 1973. Already, he had two successful offshore boats behind him. He collaborated with Ted Kaufman in designing Mercedes III for the winning Australian Admiral's Cup team of 1967. And in 1969, he designed Apollo, a 58-footer, for Alan Bond that eventually became a legendary performer under the ownership of Jack Rooklyn. He could look back on where he had been without regret or any sense of deprivation and forward with an uncanny sense of direction.

He never felt held back as a designer by lack of formal education. He had spent only two years at primary school and another two at Newcastle Junior Boys High School. He served an apprenticeship as a fitter and turner with the New South Wales railways. This gave him the metalworking skills that would later help him design and make the fittings for his America's Cup challengers. His fittings were innovative and always as light as absolutely necessary to function without failure. He once spelled out his scenario for the ideal America's Cup boat: 'So light in every way that it would fall apart and sink the moment it crossed the finishing line after winning the last race.'

His inquiring mind and vivid perception of how and why yachts sailed were the real educators. 'Sailing on a boat is the greatest teacher, analysing what characteristics the shape gives the boat in your mind,' he said. 'This way you learn from every one you sail on, as if you had designed it yourself.'

Grant Simmer, the navigator on Australia II and later design coordinator for the 2003 America's Cup winning Alinghi team, admired Lexcen since he was a teenager when Ben worked with Grant's father George on several engineering projects. They ranged from designing and making 'coffee grinder' winches for Apollo to casting magnesium alloy wheels for Ben's Ferrari because he could not afford real ones.

'The incredible thing about Ben was that if he did not understand something or could not do something, he would teach himself how it worked or physically how to do it. As an apprentice, he was trained as a fitter and turner. With a race boat, he could design the boat, do most of the boatbuilding tasks, design the most intricate mast fittings, machine the fittings, recut the sails, steer the boat, act as tactician, trim the sails, all at the level of the specialist people we employed for each job.

'As an example, in the very early days of yacht design software Ben quickly taught himself to use Maxsurf in 1987/88. As a yacht designer with his small boat and skiff background he was intuitively one of the best I have worked with.'

The ultimate dream, to design an America's Cup winner, was already implanted in 1971: 'It's no good having an inspiration in this country unless you have the money to back it up yourself because no-one has the money to spend on an experimental design,' Lexcen said. 'We just haven't got the number of customers for our own design ideas to be proven and because people aren't rich enough to gamble, they go to the overseas establishment designers like Olin Stephens.

'What always shits me off is, one day some fellow is going to win the America's Cup for Australia and it will be some guy like myself, you know. And that guy will be saying to himself, 'I could have won that 20 years ago if I had been given the opportunity.''

The ambition to win the America's Cup was already smouldering within Alan Bond. He had taken Apollo to the USA for the Newport-Bermuda race in 1970. Bond had never seen a Twelve Metre Class America's Cup boat so, while they were preparing Apollo at Bob Derecktor's City Island yard, New York, Ben took him across the dock to have a look at Valiant, the latest Olin Stephens design built for the America's Cup defence that year.

They were looking down into Valiant's cockpit when crew boss Vic Romagna came along and warned them off. Ben said: 'One day we are going to come back here with a super boat that will win the America's Cup. Then we will get a steamroller and run over it in the street outside the New York Yacht Club, so it will become the America's Plate.'

The reply became folklore. So, at the presentation of the America's Cup to the Australians in 1983, on the terrace of the William K. Vanderbilt mansion Marble House, NYYC Commodore Robert Stone presented Ben with his own trophy a squashed automobile hub cap. The ceremony was the club's most gracious gesture in a summer of acrimony over the legality of Australia II's winged keel. 'Once they lost the America's Cup, they reverted back to being normal human beings,' Lexcen said.

The America's Cup summer of 1983 and the double assault, firstly on the legality of the winged keel and whether Ben or the Dutch test-tank and wind tunnel researchers designed it, bore heavily on Lexcen, who had a history of high blood pressure. He ended up in Newport hospital – not with a heart attack as some reports had it at the time – but with some kind of murmur or irregularity. He was really just worn out and tense. The Bond syndicate decided he should stay in hospital for a few days and rest.

A day or two after he left hospital, I encountered him in the street, looking fit and in irrepressible spirits again. 'Heart attack? No, the stupid doctor hooked the cardiogram up to me back to front and it went crazy,' he said. 'I would not trust him with my pet dog.'

A great day for Ben and all present occurred during the challenger eliminations before the 1983 Cup match. Australia II returned to the dock in Newport unexpectedly early one day, its match with Britain's Victory '83 aborted by lack of wind. In the boat yard, the Australians surprised Johan Valentijn, designer of the US defender Liberty, supervising a rush job to fit a set of crude-looking wings to the keel of Freedom, Liberty's pacemaker boat.

THE LONG-RUNNING DISPUTE with NYYC over the legality of the winged keel had been terminated only a few days earlier. Ben chortled: 'They are going to have an awful lot of trouble with the New York Yacht Club trying to get it measured. It will do little more than just give the barnacles more space to grow on their boat. It's a barnacle farm. It is completely whacko. They know nothing.' He then borrowed a pencil from a newspaper reporter, signed his name on Freedom's wings, adding: 'Fifty-one out of 100 for effort.'

Alan Bond wanted to reveal the keel of Australia II to the world on September 12, the day before the America's Cup, against the wishes of Ben and others in the team who talked Bond out of it. Lexcen reasoned: 'If they see the keel is only made of lead - is not alive and does not glow – then the fright value is gone. But if you keep it hidden and beat them in an early race, they will call in the witch doctors.

'Dennis Conner (skipper of Liberty) worries. He is the most superstitious guy I have ever met. He won't sail a boat with an uneven sail number. If he believes we have something different and win a race, they'll have to tie him up.'

Ben Lexcen was so drained by the prolonged tension of the 1983 Cup match and so resigned to defeat in the deciding last race that he fell asleep aboard Australia II's tender on the second upwind leg. After Australia II won the race to decide the match, 7-6, Ben praised Conner who was reduced to tears that night. 'The whole boat speed was equal to Liberty but we were pushing to beat Dennis Conner. I tell you I was worried about Dennis Conner. He saved the Cup last time and deserves a lot of the credit for trying to save it this time. He's a tricky little devil.'

Australia II's keel was revealed after the last race; in retrospect not a good idea with defeat looming for the defender at the hands of Conner's new boat Stars & Stripes in 1987. 'When we lifted the boat tonight there were 500 Americans hanging off the keel; heaps of them, just like leeches,' Lexcen said. 'They are going to start a new religion.'

How did he feel? 'Damn relieved. It's a 12-year dream come true.'

Alan Bond, who had stuck by Lexcen as the designer through three unsuccessful challenges as well as the win, said in Newport that Ben was a genius, completely self-taught, who reminded him of an artist: 'Not all of the paintings he produces are really good. He goes through brilliant periods. He needs encouragement and I have been happy to give it to him because I recognised that he had a special quality not to be found in other people.'

BEN LEXCEN WAS a marvellous raconteur, to any audience, large or small. He was a willing speaker at sailing fund-raising and educational functions and seminars. As a boy, he was enthralled by the books of Uffa

Fox, the eccentric British genius and Nathanael Herreshoff, the famous and unconventional American designer. Later in life, he visited the homes of them both, as he told a seminar on yacht design in Sydney:

*IN AMERICA IN 1972, I went to see the boatyard of the famous designer Nat Herreshoff at Bristol, Rhode Island. His son Sidney, who was about 90 and Halsey Herreshoff (who navigated Courageous in the 1974 America's Cup and Liberty in 1983) showed me around the place, or what was left of it. Many of the buildings in the yard, which was a giant business in its heyday, were destroyed by a hurricane in the 1950s. But there was a little old house on the waterfront with a lot of the models that Captain Nat made.*

*Nat Herreshoff was an inventive old guy. He used to design with models. To take the lines off the models, he made a machine with little rack and pinions and dials and things – like a mechanical computer – so he could read off the offsets. And he had another little thing with a stylus on it that used to draw the sections of the boat. He used to race down to the boatyard and throw them to the foreman. And with a set of offsets for frame shapes he devised, which were brilliant, they would not need a construction plan and could build any yacht by this method up to 200ft and 300ft long.*

*They had a very successful business, but what I was getting down to ... it is very difficult to keep me on course ... is the difference between Nat Herreshoff and Uffa Fox. When I was a small boy, Uffa Fox was my design hero. Even though Uffa was not a very good designer, he was a great, fantastic, old storyteller and he was an observer. He wrote his books to make money. His prime aim was to get money with the least amount of work, I found out later.*

*Captain Nat was the exact opposite. He was a very industrious, inventive person. And he had these fantastic tools. When I asked old Sidney Herreshoff if I could see his tools, he opened up all these beautiful chests of chisels and planes; he had tiny little planes with which he made models.*

*I said, 'Do you think I could take one of the chisels and cut a bit of wood?' He gave me the chisel and it was like a razor; it just slipped through the wood. Then I took a bit of oil and put it where I had touched the chisel with my fingers and gave it back to him.*

*And he said, 'I've been showing people these tools for 70 years and you are the first one to ever put oil back on the chisel.' So, he took me downstairs and showed me the real stuff like the catamarans that Nat used to make that used to go straight into the wind with a big propeller instead of sails.*

*A few years later, when I lived on the Isle of Wight in England for a year, I went around to Uffa Fox's house and said, 'Where's Uffa's tools?' And they said in their Isle of Wight dialect: 'Ar, nipper, bloody Uffa didn't have any tools. He used everybody else's.'*

*So, my yacht designing hero dissolved away somewhat. But even so, his books inspired me to pursue this silly yacht designing business to the stage where I am at now ... where I am sometimes poor and sometimes rich and I struggle along.*

# 2

# FORMATIVE YEARS

*B*EN LEXCEN: THE *first thing I remember about sailing; I went down to the beach at Newcastle where the kids were racing their toy boats in a 300-metre wide rock pool. One kid's father used to make boats and the others had bought ones. I hounded my grandmother until she bought me one. It was solid Oregon, had an iron keel and when the sail got wet it used to fall on its arse. Anyhow, my boat wasn't any good so I got a bit desperate and decided to make one. If this other kid's father could make one, I could make one.*

*I read some books down at the library about model yachts by a guy called Daniels who was a famous old model yacht designer. The only tools I had were razor blades, a bunch of pins and a tube of glue. There was a model airplane shop somewhere near there and I decided to make a boat out of balsa. The first one I made was of solid balsa; expensive for me but it kept me up with the other kids.*

*The only way I could make the boats cheaper was to make them* out of sheet balsa and hollow inside. I remember this object lesson. I made a sharpie – a squared box thing – but didn't put any rocker (curvature) in the keel. I didn't know what it was. And this thing wouldn't go. It should have. It was bigger and lighter and had good sails. So I just cut the sides and put a kink in them and all of a sudden it sailed like a rocket. Suddenly I realised how important it was to have a boat designed correctly. And then my boats used to kill the other kids' boats and I never used to play boats any more.

Then I used to go and watch the boats sail on the Hunter River; the VJs on a Saturday. I was eight or nine. I eventually decided to cross the river and have a close look at them. So I got a ferry fare and away I went to the old 16ft skiff club where the VJs sailed. I was too shy to push myself in so I just watched them. Just being near them was a good thing. One day a fellow took me out for a sail. He was a real nut – I forget his name – a real Sea Scout bloke, 'avast' and 'belay' and everything else. He yelled at me all the way but I was as happy as Larry because I went out in a damned boat.

In the meantime, a friend of mine, a kid called Eddie Harvey and I used to go down to the wharves fishing where the fishermen would leave their boats. We'd pinch their rowing boats and take a broom and a flour bag and blow around the harbour, then put the boat back ... and get abused every now and again. We'd go down to Lake Macquarie, hire a six-metre canoe for a couple of hours, take a sail with us and stick it up once we had paddled around the corner from the hire place.

There was a move to start the 16ft skiffs again at the Hunter River Sailing Club. They had raced there before the war. The old fellows who used to sail them decided to get them going again and came around looking for crew. They got on their push bikes and rode all over Stockton looking for the blokes who used to sail the skiffs before the war. I decided to join them and started sailing on this 16ft skiff called Adele, which was 24 years old ... you could see through it. After chucking lumps of water over the side of this skiff for a couple of years I started sailing on another skiff there as second forward hand or something.

Then a yacht came into Newcastle, on a cruise to Port Stephens. I think it was called Thea but I've never been able to find anything about it. It tied up among the ships. The guys were filling it with water. They let me look over it and I helped them put the water on. I begged them to take me to Port Stephens.

'Your mother wouldn't like it,' they said.

*'She said I could go.' (I was going to walk back from Port Stephens.)*
*But they didn't take me. I followed them on my bike on the breakwater,*
*all the way out to the bay. I had never seen a yacht for real before; only*
*photographs.*

BEN LEXCEN WAS born Bob Miller, in 1936, at Boggabri, an outback
town in the state of New South Wales. He had a tough, disrupted, childhood. His father Edward, 21, was a timber cutter working with the NSW
government railways, in gangs deep in the bush, supplying the hardwood sleepers that carried the rails. These were hard times, at the tail of
the Great Depression. Bob and his mother Doreen moved from camp to
camp with Edward Miller following the work, living in tents. He recalled
visiting the pubs with his father who would spend his last penny on
shouting drinks for the bar, running up accounts and then having to
leave town because he couldn't pay them.

The marriage was unhappy, with violent fights. Ben told 1984 biog-
rapher Bruce Stannard: 'He didn't like my mother but he liked me.' It
ended at the start of World War Two when Edward left them to join the
Air Force. 'He came home for half an hour. I remember his grey-blue
uniform and his piercing blue eyes. He had a fight with my mother and I
never saw him again.' Ben believed his father had found another woman.
He was obviously fond of his father and told me once that he had later
gone looking for him.

Doreen Miller, who was good looking, found work as a barmaid in
the bush towns and later in Sydney. 'The war was on and there were lots
of American soldiers around,' Miller told Stannard. 'I was a nuisance to
her, so she dumped me with her sisters. I did the rounds of all the aun-
ties, all five of them. When one got sick of me, she would dump me on
the next. I never knew where I was.'

Eventually, aged seven, he went to live with his grandparents in Newcastle. After his grandmother died, his grandfather Mick Taylor looked
after him.

BEN LEFT SCHOOL at the age of 14 to become an apprentice fitter
and turner with the NSW railways in Newcastle. He had begun school
at nine, spending two years at Bolton Street Primary School and then
another two years at Newcastle Junior Boys' High School. Although he
regretted that later, he never felt his lack of formal education had held
him back as a yacht designer or as a person with a well-rounded intellect

who, besides his passion for sailing boats and later fast cars, became a connoisseur of classical music and art. His research into model yachts at the public library taught him the greatest lessons of all, seldom acquired short of university – how and where to find out about subjects that really interested him.

'I look at a lot of books but never read the bloody things,' he told me in the early 1970s.

Was that a drawback? 'No, I think it is an advantage as you are not inhibited. I was lousy at maths at school. I hated school. But if I see something interesting in a book, I read it.'

He wanted to become an apprentice boatbuilder approaching builders of rowing shells, lifeboats, even the state dockyard in Newcastle, as well as the yacht builders, but could not get a start because he did not have the intermediate certificate from school. However, the fitter and turner apprenticeship was valuable. Later, he was to use the technical drawing and metal-working skills he acquired at the railways to fashion innovative and complex fittings for yachts – eventually Alan Bond's Australian America's Cup challengers.

*I WENT TO Lake Macquarie to see the yachts finishing a race from Sydney, at Easter. Wings, the 30 Square Metre, won it so I whizzed home, got my balsa and made models of 30 square metres. And then I made a beaut model of this Daniels design from a magazine – a Marblehead class. It was so fast, I couldn't run from one end of the pool to the other before it would bash into the other end.*

*The pool down at the beach wasn't big enough so I went down to the railway station and caught the old train that used to go to Belmont once a day. I sailed it there and met a kid who let me leave it at his house so I didn't have to lug it backwards and forwards. I made another one I designed myself. He would sail one and I'd sail the other, steering with cotton tied on the tiller. Eventually I had half a dozen of them, with half a dozen kids racing up and down and I would be trying things out on them all the time.*

*Uffa Fox was my inspiration. I used to read his books because they had good pictures in them. I was certainly impressed by his sailing the canoe across the English Channel and all that sort of thing. I used to read these books with beautiful old boats in them. I used to make models of the old cutters like Shamrock with their topsails and long bowsprits. They were made of balsa and used to go like rockets with the big*

Star fleet Bayview, 1956
RYVES FAMILY ARCHIVE

*sails, most times reaching.*

*Then one day I got a ride on a Vee Ess at Belmont. The owner was in the merchant navy, used to go away a lot and I used to sail his rotten old boat when he wasn't there. It was real heavy but I was happy as ... I didn't care if I never finished. Eventually, he decided to give sailing away and gave me the boat. So, I had this old boat, called Rendezvous. I kept it for a few years and I decided to build myself a little yacht.*

*I built this 20ft yacht in this guy's back yard. I didn't have any money so I didn't put anything in it to make it strong; no frames. They'd say, 'It's not strong enough' and I'd say, 'it is strong enough, it's all scientifically worked out'. As I cast the lead for the keel, the lead exploded and went all over the bloody backyard. I gave the Vee Ess to another kid who used to crew a lot.*

THE YACHT, NAMED Comet, was undoubtedly fast. Then, as now, there were many fast keelboats on Lake Macquarie – a wonderful recreational waterway just south of Newcastle. It's a deeply indented lagoon of the sea, four times as big as Sydney Harbour but with very little rise and fall of tide, offering not only good racing courses in flat water on its wider expanses but also great day sailing and overnight cruising, with many secluded anchorages on its 174 km of largely bush-covered shoreline.

The 16-year-old Bob Miller both cruised and raced on the lake with Comet for several years. The boat was hard chine, had an aft-sloping transom, a separate spade rudder and was certainly ahead of its time – on the lake at least. 'It was like a square Soling,' Miller said. 'It was terrific on the wind; it used to burn all the big boats off. I could beat the

30 square metres in light weather.'

Miller enjoyed cruising around the lake, often alone. He raced it only now and again and repairing it most of the time. 'Gee I had some trouble with that bloody boat but it was fun,' he said. 'It wouldn't tip over and you could go sailing by yourself.'

His sailing – and life – changed direction when the Star class keelboats gathered at Lake Macquarie for a regatta one Easter. He tried to pace them with Comet. 'I thought I will burn these bastards off but they were too fast, had too much sail. I could beat them when it was blowing.'

Star Pineapple; Carl Ryves steering with Steve Auland, racing on Sydney Harbour
RYVES FAMILY ARCHIVE

One of the Star class sailors from Sydney, Joe Adams – who years later was to join Bob in the Miller & Whitworth yacht design team – was impressed by Comet and by Bob. 'We got friendly and he said, 'Why don't you come down to Sydney and sail in the Stars. You can live at my place if you come down,' Miller recalled.

'I said, 'Oh yeah, that's a good idea.' I bought an old motor bike just to ride down and I went down to Sydney one weekend. It took me four attempts to get there. Joe, who lived at Punchbowl, drove me around in his old Armstrong Siddley. We went to Pittwater where the Stars were hanging up (on davits).'

There, Bob met Ted Kaufman, preparing a new Star for the 1956 Olympic Games trials. Kaufman was having trouble with the leeward runner washing aft while the boat was sailing to windward. Miller, back in Newcastle, as a 'foreign order' at the railways made some clips that would automatically hold the slack runner forward and gave them to Kaufman next time he drove to Sydney on his old and unregistered motor bike.

Bob Miller and Carl Ryves on Carl's
Flying Dutchman Sidewinder, 1958
RYVES FAMILY ARCHIVE

Kaufman, impressed, invited Miller to crew for him. Now sailing both days of the weekend with Kaufman, Miller got a transfer to Sydney with the railways, continuing to live with Joe Adams at Punch-bowl. In-fighting between the Sydney competitors and disagreements with Kaufman eventually made Miller's Star-sailing experience an unhappy one. They were eventually beaten at the Olympic trials in Melbourne by locals Bob French and Jack Downey.

But through the Stars, Miller met the next major influences on his life, Carl Ryves and the Ryves family. Ryves' father Jim had built himself a Star in the backyard of his home at Hunter's Hill. He was short of money and apparently experience in dealing with competitors in what was then a cutthroat class. He built the Star from Oregon and hardwood while the others were building their boats from the expensive and difficult to obtain cedar. 'So, it floated three inches lower in the water than a normal Star,' said Carl Ryves. His parents cruised around the harbour in the Star on Sundays and Carl would race it on Saturdays in a newly-formed Sydney Harbour Star fleet based on the Lane Cove River near the Ryves family home at Hunters Hill.

Carl Ryves had first met Bob Miller before the 1956 Olympic trials while he was crewing for Ted Kaufman and living in Newcastle. 'I was 14 and he was 19,' Ryves says. He had an unregistered 'beesa', BSA motor bike. I don't think it had lights. I know he didn't have a licence and he used to ride down from Newcastle on Friday night, sail with Kaufman and then go back to work at the railways on Monday morning.

After the Olympic trials, Bob began crewing occasionally for Ryves on the Star Pineapple, which Miller remembered as, 'A great big heavy box with dirty old cotton sails.' Then Jim and Carl Ryves, encouraged by Lloyd Burgess, secretary of the Royal Sydney Yacht Squadron, began to build a Flying Dutchman dinghy – newly chosen as an Olympic class – at their home. 'During that time Benny had moved to Sydney on a transfer in the railways and he worked at Chullora, which was great for foreign orders. You could get anything made out there,' Carl Ryves recalled.

'We started to build a Flying Dutchman, my father and I. Benny had begun building a Mark II Moth. The Moths had only a beam, sail area and length measurement, so Benny's one was very Uffa Fox influenced with a deep forefoot. From the front of the centreboard case back was really straight. It's as though it was made out of match sticks, with tiny plywood gussets and things. He had that half built somewhere, it could have been at Joe Adams' house and then he moved the whole contraption and himself to our place. And he just seemed to finish up there. The Moth appeared, then his clothes.'

Ben adopted the Ryves family. The house was never locked and Mrs Ryves found him there one morning sleeping on the sofa. After this happened on a few occasions, the Ryves' set up a camp bed for him in the shed in the back garden. He ate with them in the house. 'He seemed very happy there and lived with us for four or five years,' Carl said. 'My parents were very good to him and our house was full of action with lots of visitors, interesting friends of my parents and kids galore.'

Hunters Hill in those days was not an enclave for the rich and famous as it tends to be now. The community included

Sidewinder carried home-made sails
RYVES FAMILY ARCHIVE

27

Above: Bob Miller (left) and Carl Ryves
with the Dicko Cup, won with Sidewinder
at Royal Prince Alfred's annual social
race for a mixed fleet on Pittwater
Below: Sidewinder car-topped,
heading for Lake Macquarie, about
1958 / RYVES FAMILY ARCHIVE

many musicians, artists and art lovers. Among the Ryves' neighbours were Hardmuth ('Hottie') Lahm, a well-known black and white artist who used to draw Snifter in Man magazine and Snowy McGann in the Sun Herald, the cartoonist WEP (William Edwin Pidgeon) and Hal Missingham, director of the Art Gallery of New South Wales.

THE SHED IN the backyard was a busy place too, with boat building and car building going on and a separate photographic darkroom. The house was full of records and books, including a set of pre-war Uffa Fox books on yacht design. 'Benny read those books on our lounge floor for three or four hours every night and studied the pictures of the Herreshoff boats and Nicholson boats and their fittings,' Carl said. 'He would look at the fittings and suggest improved ways of doing things so that everything was minimum weight.

'Ben really enjoyed all these things, listening to rock, jazz and classical music on my father's fantastic sound system, with sand-filled speakers that weighed half a ton each and reading everything, including huge volumes of encyclopaedias,' Carl Ryves said. 'He entertained us with his antics, astounded us with his general knowledge and had an amazing ability to make everything in the workshop.'

One of Bob Miller's many eccentricities at the Ryves house was playing the harmonica under the shower. He liked the acoustics there. Drip-dry synthetic fibres had just been introduced. 'He used to stand in the shower washing his clothes and playing the mouth organ, then just walk out down the road to dry out,' Ryves said. 'For a time, he had only one pair of trousers. He would wash them by standing in them, under the shower and then walked in them around until they were dry.'

Bob and Carl had a huge influence on each other. They built boats together, sailed them on the bush-lined serpentine Lane Cove River near the Ryves family home and on Sydney Harbour beyond and shared rich life-learning experiences ashore.

Bob Miller's Moth, steered by Carl Ryves, about 1960
RYVES FAMILY ARCHIVE

First, Carl helped Bob finish building the Moth which had gates – small wings on the rudder – to prevent cavitation bubble drag and then sailed it a lot on the river. 'We used to do crazy things like putting my ten-year-old brother Mike on it, in a black nor'easter to see how fast it could go,' Ryves said. 'I would sail the Moth to the top of the river, Benny and Mike would sail the Star up. Then we'd put Mike on the Moth with instructions to stay head to wind for a while. We'd run half way down the river with the Star so Benny could to see how the Moth would plane along with Mike on it, weighing only around four stone. And Mike would go roaring down the river, get to the end of it and just capsize.'

By then, Miller had left the railways and gone to work for Peter Cole, the talented sailmaker and yacht designer at Balmain, riding the ferry there from Hunters Hill. He used to sail with Cole on Cole's self-designed Avenger. 'It was a little moulded ply thing,' Miller recalled. 'Peter was my hero for a long time because he was a great Vee Ess sailor and I'd had a Vee Ess.'

He helped the Ryves build the Flying Dutchman. They were short of money and Miller made most of the fittings: gooseneck, rudder gudgeons and every block and pulley on the boat. 'He spliced all the rigging and made all the fittings for the wooden mast; generally better

Above: Carl steering Bob's catamaran,
filled with family and friends
Below: Bob's catamaran

than everyone else's. They had great big mast tangs where his were really neat and slippery little things. And rather than 20 bolts through the mast, we had the end of the tang bent down into a tiny little cut in the mast.

'Then Benny and I, but mainly he, made the sails for the boat on Mum's sewing machine. By then he had left Peter Cole. He worked there for less than a year.'

Jim Ryves suggested that they call the FD Sidewinder. He had read about the Sidewinder missile the Americans were using in the Korean war against the Russian-built MIGs. 'We were told it was just a bit of water pipe with a bomb in the end of it,' said Carl. 'It was cheap, it was fast and it was dangerous. That started the snake thing with Benny then building the Taipan and Venom.'

Together, they also built a 20ft catamaran from scrap timber in two weeks. At the time they were fascinated by all things Hawaiian; favouring loud Hawaiian shirts and hats and they'd seen pictures of the famous Manu Kai catamaran on the beach at Waikiki. 'We built it rough and quick in the backyard at my father's house,' said Carl. 'When Benny became impatient at the rate of progress, he would kick it and once tried to set fire to it.

'The water was three-quarters of a mile away so we got a dozen friends, carried it down the road and launched it over the wall. We got the mast from an old 18-footer and the mainsail from my FD, which hadn't been launched yet. We didn't have the rudders made. Ben was steering it with a sweep oar over the back in quite a fresh nor'easter and I was sitting hanging onto the mainsheet on the leeward hull, making it sink down. Anyhow, the thing started flying – it went like a rocket – and after five minutes capsized. When it was finished we used to race the ferries with it; sail it up to Redleaf Beach and take the bikini girls sailing.'

Miller said of the project: 'I had a mad idea about cats being marvellous boats. I built this bloody awful cat really, but it would go. Carl and I would sail it all over the harbour. We raced the ferry, capsized it occasionally and broke a couple of masts.' Later, Miller designed a 25ft catamaran for Ryves; a very pretty boat which Ryves sailed around the harbour for a couple of years. He also designed a bigger one, around 30-35ft long, which went to the Whitsundays and sailed as a resort cat for 20 years. 'He did it all by eye, all by guess; not by mathematics,' said Ryves.

Ryves saw Hawaii for the first time in 1962, on his way back from sailing in a Dragon class world championship in Europe with Norman Booth. 'It was like going to Mecca. I bought these shorts with Royal Hawaiian on them – Benny subsequently wore his for the next 10 years – Hawaiian shirts and pictures of Manu Kai.'

Miller raced at times with Ryves on the Flying Dutchman. The regular crew was Steve Auland but on Sundays, Ryves and Miller would cruise around the harbour on the Flying Dutchman, heading for the popular picnic anchorage Quarantine, or the Redleaf beach in Double Bay, to 'chat up' the bikini-clad girls and take them sailing. And they used to race the 18-footers. 'They had huge sails and in those days crews up to six with five on the wire and the skipper steering – Cliffie Monkhouse, Lennie Heffernan and all those guys,' Ryves says. 'We used to start a bit behind in reasonable nor'easter and we'd beat them to the Sow and Pigs in a dead beat to windward by hundreds of yards. The 18s were a bit faster than us downwind, but not by much except in dead light weather.'

Miller sailed the long, light and lean Flying Dutchmen on and off for more than ten years and their influence on his designs can be seen from the 18ft skiffs to the Contender trapeze-powered one-man dinghy and eventually Alan Bond's ocean racer Apollo, labelled by Ryves as a '57ft FD'. Ryves and Auland won the NSW championship in their first season in the Flying Dutchman class with their Bob Miller home-made sails. Two seasons later, they finished third in the Australian championship on Sydney Harbour, won by Victorian Noel Brooke from Jim O'Grady (WA) in a strong fleet of about 45 boats.

The line-up included the noted Brisbane 18ft skiff skipper Norm Wright in a German-built boat, A.S.Huybers. 'Norman Wright saw how fast we were with Ben Lexcen sails on a home-made boat sailed by a couple of kids; we were 17 then where most Flying Dutchman sailors were in their 30s,' Ryves recalls. 'So Norman Wright said to Benny, 'Seeing you are unemployed at present, having left the railways and Peter Cole, come to Brisbane and we'll modify a building above the boat yard and form a partnership to start a sail loft.' I remember going out to the train with Benny and a girl he was very fond of but she wasn't so fond of him as he had tears in his eyes and she didn't. But he did have that drawing book under his arm,' said Ryves.

Ryves and Miller kept in touch. 'We used to write to each other every month,' Ryves says. 'He subsequently made us a new set of sails to take to the Olympic trials in Melbourne in 1959 and we came third in those – Rolly Tasker won, Noel Brooke was second and we came third with the only set of Ben Lexcen (Bob Miller) sails in the fleet, which I thought was pretty good. We hardly knew where the wind was coming from, were half the age of most of the competitors and Tasker was world champion.'

Bob Miller was 21, the year 1958, when he moved to Brisbane and set up Flo-Rite sails in a loft above the Wright family's renowned boat-building shed on the Brisbane River. It was tougher going than Miller had expected with few big-boat customers, but he worked hard making sails for the FDs and other dinghy classes and was good with the customers, patiently talking through their boat-speed and tuning problems.

Two years later, with the business going well, Miller fell 45ft from a yacht mast, survived, but for six weeks lay in hospital with a fractured vertebrae, pelvis, finger and splintered heel. The fall marked the real beginning of the career as a yacht designer that was 23 years later to win the America's Cup.

# 3

# THE RADICAL 18S

B EN LEXCEN IN THE EARLY 1960s, while he was working as a
sailmaker for Brisbane boatbuilder Norman Wright, inspired by
his experience in the Flying Dutchman class, designed, built and sailed
two radical for the time 18ft skiffs that eventually transformed the class
from traditional open-boat, large sail carriers manned by five or more
crew members to the three-handed trapeze-powered speedsters that
attract healthy spectator followings not only on Sydney Harbour but in
Auckland, New Zealand; the USA and Europe. He describes how it happened:

> NORM WRIGHT WAS a good bloke for me because he never put the
> kibosh on any idea I would ever have. No matter how mad it was he
> would always encourage me. And it was a great thing for me. Craig
> (Whitworth) is good, but he's too practical. Everything has got to work
> before you start doing it so he tends to throw cold water on a lot of

Bob Miller steering Taipan
AUSTRALIAN 18-FOOTERS LEAGUE ARCHIVE

*the things and it tends to make me lethargic all the time. So, I think, 'What's the bloody good; it won't work, won't make a profit.' Whereas Norman Wright would say, 'Oh Jesus, that's a bloody good idea, we'll do that,' and start talking the possibilities over with you in a really enthusiastic way and take them to the extreme all the time. Everything I thought of, he would never chuck cold water on it, no matter how crazy it was.*

*One day when I was measuring a mast for a sail I fell off and hurt myself badly. I climbed up this bloody mast on a 45-footer to see where the black band was and make sure the measuring tape was dead on it. I* had pulled the tape up with the main halyard and tied it off on a cleat. I put a shackle on the end of the main halyard so I could take it back down again with me but didn't tie the rope (to pull the halyard back down) to the shackle.

I just tied it on with a piece of Venetian blind cord, as the rope was too thick to go through the shackle. I forgot this. I was coming back down the mast and got to the second set of cross trees. It was a bit awkward and I grabbed this rope to heave myself up a bit to get my leg over the cross trees and the blind cord broke. I just lost my grip and fell down.

I was in hospital for three months. I was really crook. Norm was great. He made a drawing board for me I could use in bed and brought magazines for me. I virtually drew Taipan (Miller's first 18ft skiff) while I was in hospital. I told Norm I was going to build a three-man 18-footer. Norm said, 'You should make a model before you build a boat, always, to look at,' which was good. He glued me up a lump of wood and I made the model. He showed me a few things that would be difficult to build in plywood as it couldn't be bent. Norm, who was world and Australian 18-footer champion, probably didn't believe it would be any good. I loved the Flying Dutchman but he had one and I thought there was no point in me having one and I was looking for something else to sail up there.

He was always talking about the 18-footers and it was infectious. So, I said, 'Why can't we make an 18-footer like a Dutchman? There's nothing in the rules to say you can't.' He could beat the 18-footers with his Dutchman on the wind. 'Let's make it for three blokes with two on trapeze.' And he said, 'Oh, that's a terrific idea', and he might have thought it wouldn't work, either. But at least he didn't say so. So, I did it. It didn't cost much. We got old Klinki ply, he had all the tools there to make a boat and I could make it quick. I was going to make it so light, with the keel really thin – the keel doesn't have to be any stronger than the rest of the boat, why couldn't it be made from thin plywood? He said, 'No reason why you can't', but showed me a few pitfalls. So, I made the keel out of 5/16in ply and all the frames out of 3/16in plywood. The stringers sat on top of the plywood, the frames didn't touch the bottom of the boat.

Norm said I had to use a grown ti-tree knee in the stem. It was out of the same bit of wood from which he'd built the stem for his last 18-footer Jenny; he wanted something old-fashioned. So, I rabetted it all out. It was a bit rough but it was good for me. He made me a *mast of Bunyah pine. It was light, only 25lb or something – he was really enthused – and the spinnaker pole weighed about five pounds. We weren't going for big spinnakers. We figured we could burn these bastards off with the weight advantage.*

*The first race day came. I didn't have a mainsail but borrowed Norm's Flying Dutchman mainsail, which was ridiculous. They all took off and left me for last and eventually the rudder gudgeon broke. They all laughed and were poking shit at me. I really got my mad up and that week I worked like mad and strengthened the boat with the help of Norm who said, 'You made everything too light, you have to think of it being strong.' So, we went all over it and made everything stronger - he wouldn't tell me first but he let me do it first and find out for myself. I made a mainsail for it, next weekend came and we just pissed off; so far in front you couldn't see another boat on a full reach of the river.*

*That year I did all right, winning practically all the races up there on fastest time except sometimes, when there was a bad ebb tide, the other boats would eventually catch me with their ringtails and bigger spinnakers on the longer course. I made some really terrific spinnakers for the Sharpie class at that time – like Herbulot cut ones – that could be carried really shy. So, I made a giant Sharpie spinnaker for the 18-footer except it was masthead and double luff (where the other 18s carried asymmetric spinnakers) and developed a way of gybing it really fast. It was like a piece of Danish furniture that boat.*

THE HULL OF Taipan, hard-chine and built with 3/16in plywood bottom and 1/8in plywood topsides, weighed only about 100 lb where the normal planked, round-bilge 18s of those days weighed 600 lb. The philosophy of Uffa Fox, that weight was useful only in a steam roller, was obvious in the Taipan design. It had reverse sheer instead of the traditional concave sheerline profile and canoe bow with the stem only 12in to 14in deep. It was originally drawn with a normal stem but changed with a typical Miller whim. The Wrights and Bob were sitting down having breakfast one morning when he jumped up and left the table. 'They could hear this sawing going on and when Norm goes out to have a look, he'd sawn the bow off and put a reverse sheer in the boat,' recalls Len Heffernan, sailing opponent and later good friend of Miller's.

The rig, inspired by the Flying Dutchman class, featured an overlapping genoa and the masthead double-luffed spinnaker. Crewed by Miller, young Norm Wright (son of Norm Wright Jr) and Brian Hamil-

Taipan draws the crowd at the Georges River SC skiff challenge
RYVES FAMILY ARCHIVE

ton, Taipan finished second in the Australian championship in that first season (1959-60) to Len Heffernan's Jantzen Girl from Sydney. Heffernan, who had also won the Australian championship the previous year, was one of the most astute 18-footer sailors of that era who designed and built his own boats and many skiffs for others and certainly had a good appreciation of the qualities that made boats fast. He was immediately sold on the potential of the Taipan-style three-handers. 'It was so fast on the wind,' he said. 'What Bobbie Miller had done was to achieve the breakthrough with his power-to-weight ratio and Taipan would plane on the wind. Our boats would get up and plane downwind, but Taipan was the first that could actually plane on the wind in the right conditions. But the spinnakers were too small. It only had one spinnaker pole, 8ft long or something while ours was 24ft. In very light conditions we were too fast for it on the Brisbane River.'

Taipan was so different to the traditional 18s, it drew immediate fire from the 18-footer establishment. Later that year, when Jantzen Girl and Taipan went to Auckland for the 1960 J.J.Giltinan world championship as the only Australian representatives, at the insistence of the Sydney delegates, the race committee made Miller cut big holes in the foredeck and side decks to meet the class definition of an 'open boat'. This reduced the decked area by 14 square feet. The ruling was costly for Miller because the deck was a structural element of Taipan, stopping it from twisting. It greatly reduced the stiffness of the hull structure and left it to ship water in the choppy waters of the Waitemata.

Miller said: 'The rules said it had to be a half-decked boat; which meant a boat with a bit of deck on it. But they took it to mean half the area could be decked and no more. The deck was the only thing holding this boat together. Without the deck it would just fall to bits, just a bundle of plywood.'

Taipan was up against boats carrying lee cloths, right up to the mast, which were effective in keeping out the water slopped in by the short, tide-ridden chop of the Waitemata Harbour while Miller wasn't even allowed to rig a lee cloth.

New Zealander Bernie Skinner's Surprise, a very light multi-chined plywood boat built by Dave Marks, won with 1-1-3-2-1 placings from two other Auckland boats, Vindicator (Jim Lidgard) and Ace Hi (John Lasher). Heffernan and Miller both had bad luck in that series which, says Heffernan, either could have won. Taipan finished fourth, winning one race and breaking her mast in another two, but the boat showed great potential with the ability to plane on the wind.

Practically all competitors suffered mishaps and the series was undecided until the final two heats. Heffernan capsized while three-quarters of a mile ahead in one race and was disqualified from the last race after finishing first. That would have secured Jantzen Girl second place in the series but she was disqualified on a third-party protest by a race official. In pulling away on port tack to clear the right-of-way starboard tack Surprise soon after the start, Jantzen Girl touched the end of Surprise's boom.

Miller recalled: 'On the first day, it was blowing, I was killing them on the wind but there was a big ebb tide on Auckland Harbour and every wave we went over would fill the boat with water. By some miracle, we didn't capsize and came third. The next day, there wasn't so much sea, medium wind and we just killed them and won.

'We had lousy spinnakers. I hadn't the experience to know and I was always frightened of big spinnakers. We were always getting beaten downwind. And I was too green, hadn't had enough experience in 18s and was getting into trouble all the time in the race. I came back with my tail between my legs, vowing that next time I would make a super boat that would just wipe them out.'

Taipan, restored for the Australian National Maritime Museum, launching November 2008, steered by John Bertrand with Carl Ryves and Dick Sargeant / ROSS

Len Heffernan returned from Auckland with a vow, too – to campaign to have the Taipan-style three-handers accepted by the two Sydney 18-footer clubs. Heffernan and Miller became good friends in Auckland. After the racing they swapped boats. Heffernan was impressed by the three-hander; Miller on his return to shore with Jantzen Girl said to Heffernan: 'How do you sail that thing?'

Heffernan tried to get his home club, the Sydney Flying Squadron, to admit the three-handers to its racing but the old timers, like 'Wee Georgie' Robinson, wanting to retain the open-boat spirit of the older 18s with their massive sail plans and numerous crew, strongly resisted the move. So, Heffernan built a compromise four-hander boat for the following season's racing while Miller built Venom.

*I WENT BACK to Brisbane and tried to build this super boat, Manfred Curry all round and streamlined. I was so anxious to build it, I drew it out full-sized on the loft floor – I couldn't be bothered drawing plans – and started to make it. Because it hadn't been planned, it took me forever to make it. For every step I came to, there was a problem because I hadn't allowed for it. Eventually Norm finished it. I got sick of it.*

*We called this one Venom and this was a super boat. We won our first race by miles and we just kept winning. I made this Sharpie spinnaker, but it wasn't that big, out of three-quarter-ounce cloth for the world championship on the river. Craig Whitworth was sailing with Norm Wright's son (also named Norman Wright) and me then. We went around to see the Sydney boats and to me they looked faster and better than ours with big sails and pretty good quality too. I really had the shits up and Craig kept saying, 'They're no good, we'll kill them.'*

*Before I went to New Zealand I was over-confident. This time I was beaten before I started. Anyhow the first heat came and we got out on the river with this spinnaker we had never used before. Lennie Heffernan had a ring tail and I thought, 'Downwind, he is going to kill us.'*

*We were waiting for the start, all sitting in the bottom of the boat relaxing, when a bloody puff came along and the boat capsized, filled with water and sank, about ten minutes before the start. I didn't know what to do with the boats all milling around. Craig joins the spinnaker braces together and swims for the shore. He's swimming away and Normy Wright and I are swimming, trying to tow it towards the beach and the current is washing us down river.*

*We let more rope go and eventually Craig begins floundering and*

Len Heffernan, Jack Hamilton and a model for a magazine photoshoot, sail Venom
AUSTRALIAN 18-FOOTERS LEAGUE

*sinks so we have to pull him back to the boat and get on the rope and swim ourselves. We got into the mud and bailed her out. All the boats are gone, out of sight around the bend in the river. We took off after them and came third. It was blowing like hell and we caught up. They disqualified us for getting outside assistance because Craig jumped on the shore and grabbed a bucket from a guy and bailed the boat out.*

So the next heat came, over a southeast course. Lennie Heffernan and I were battling it out on the wind. I didn't get a very good start and had to pass all the boats upwind. Then it was a tight reach and a square run after a bend in the river. We got on this really tight reach, both going like the hammers. He had this really flat spinnaker on for the shy reach. We were keeping up with him with our little flat spinnaker. We got to the bend and I thought, 'Boy, this is where we change to our magic spinnaker'.

We square up ... pshew ... down with this spinnaker and up with the big one ... phooboom ... it filled and I thought, 'Right, we're through him.' But he's done the same thing, pulled his flat one down and put up a giant spinnaker and put the ringtail out. But we went away from his just the same and won that.

When I first started sailing 18-footers I was a 20-year-old kid and the 18-footer sailors of those days were 40-year-old and 35-year-old strong men. They were always talking about the olden days when Joe Blow used to jump on board the other boat and beat someone over the head with a tiller. On the Brisbane River I actually raced against an 18 with the last of the ringtails. Nobody had seen one for ten years and until Len Heffernan re-introduced a modern version of this big sail that went up behind the mainsail. It really was effective and a Brisbane skipper copied Len.

We were leading a race to the finish and this guy caught up with this great big ringtail in light weather. He went past to windward and as I was trying to luff him out, his rig brushed against our boat. I said to my crew: 'Grab hold of his boat and hang onto it.' We hung on and were getting a real ride along to leeward of him with our bow still sticking out in front.

We thought this old guy, who used to tell me stories about the olden-day fighting, would take it in good part but he got really upset and threatened to punch us. His whole crew was leaning into the boat to try and get us. And when they did that, their boat would go to capsize and I would pull away to make it more likely to. They would have to get back up to windward to stop capsizing, get mad again and rush in to try and grab us again. Eventually, we couldn't hang on any more for laughing and they went past us.

Then, to add insult from injury, we got a big puff from behind and zoomed across to windward to win the race. They wouldn't let us come ashore. We had to sail down the Brisbane River to near the abattoirs and walk home.

VENOM WON THE remaining three races in the 1960-61 J.J.Giltinan Trophy series on the Brisbane River by margins of up to ten minutes to win the series with a total of 400 points from Heffernan's Jantzen Girl (1-2-ret-2-3, 298.87) and Queenslander MG III (Harold Watts), 2-4-2-4-5, 237.82.

The boat was as much a breakthrough in 18-footer design as the winged keel of the America's Cup winner Australia II in 1983. It was to send the 18s down the path towards lighter, smaller, boats and crews with more efficient sail plans but even more exciting performance. It was very much influenced by advanced dinghies and small keelboats designed by the German sailor Manfred Curry, who was a leading sailing theorist in the 1930s with streamlined topsides, rounded gunwales and low stem. It had a lot of balsa in the hull structure and Miller

Above: Venom's radical hull lines.
Below: The hull was a lightweight
AUSTRALIAN 18-FOOTERS LEAGUE

even made a balsa rudder for it with end plates on the bottom to solve the problem of drag caused by tip vortex – disturbed water around the bottom of the rudder – and little gates on the leading edge to stop air sucking down it to cause inefficient cavitation.

Miller also tried an end-plate on the bottom of the centreboard but had to remove it when it began collecting jelly fish and because of the difficulty of inserting from the bottom of the boat. 'So, when the Dutch and the Yanks said Benny didn't design that keel, they were wrong,' said Carl Ryves. 'He did. The principles were firmly in his mind all those years before.'

Ryves recalls sailing Taipan in a challenge race with other 18s and 16ft skiffs at the Georges River Sailing Club with bookmakers on the shore in 1959. The first prize was 75 pounds; a large amount of money at a time when the basic wage was 15 pounds a week. 'For some reason Benny couldn't make it and I sailed the boat for him with his two crew, Norman Wright Jr and Bunny Hamilton.

'It was in a 15-18 knot nor'easter and by the time we got to the first windward mark we were a couple of minutes ahead. It was the first time I'd been out on it. I wouldn't let the crew set the spinnaker on the reaches or the runs because I didn't want it to capsize. I think we won the race by eight minutes. The thing was light years ahead of any other 18-footer around. The manager down there (Frank Scott) was about to give me the 75 quid when Jenny Wright grabbed the money and it went straight into the handbag. I don't think Benny ever saw it, but the Wrights probably owned half the boat, or all the boat, anyway.'

After Venom's J.J.Giltinan win, Georges River again decided to stage a match race during the winter, which Venom won from Jantzen Girl. This may or may not have been the race Miller remembered: 'I bought the boat down to Sydney one weekend and the Sydney people on the ferry threw beer bottles and beer cans at me and said, 'Take it back to Queensland.' I slayed them sailing with some bloke who had never sailed before in his life and Carl and we beat them by 20 minutes or something.'

Miller then linked up with Craig Whitworth to sail the Flying Dutchman A.S.Huybers, which had been presented to the Royal Queensland Yacht Squadron by its philanthropic commodore Alf Huybers. 'I gave the 18-footers away because there was no point in doing anything else with them. I'd proved my point. I didn't love sailing them; they were rotten to sail really because they had no rules and used to run their races like horse racing ... 'Come up so and so' on the starting line and that sort of thing.'

Whitworth was a steadying influence on Venom. He had been a top Gwen 12 dinghy sailor and Miller had made his sails. He was a completely practical person and used to make the regular lists of tasks that

Venom / AUSTRALIAN 18-FOOTERS LEAGUE ARCHIVE

needed doing on the boat; making sure it did not break. 'Craig was really good for Benny,' Carl Ryves says. 'He got the boat sorted out; made it stronger, put decent shackles on where Benny had light shackles because of his lightness fetish.'

Whitworth said Norm Wright asked him to sail on Venom because Taipan, although very fast, had kept breaking down. 'My job on Venom was to prepare the boat, be working back at night checking the gear,' he said. 'It was a great design and we held it together that way. I was the technician.

'WHILE WE WOULD win every race quite easily, Bob would need only a little thing to go wrong or annoy him and he would just blow. We were going back up the river one day; the boat was very light with little plywood floorboard slats. Bob caught his toe in one of them. 'These so and so things,' he said and began ripping them out. He pulled out three sets of floorboards with his bare hands while he was sailing the boat. I was out on the wire. I couldn't do anything. I was just laughing; to was so stupid. He was just absolutely volatile.'

Meanwhile in Sydney, Lennie Heffernan worked on courageously against some bitter opposition to have the Miller three-hander legacy taken up by the 18s. By the time he had the three-handers accepted by the Sydney Flying Squadron, it was September, too late to build one for the new season. Miller wanted Heffernan to have Venom and towed it on a trailer to Sydney for him.

Heffernan and his crew Jack Hamilton were, however, able to sail it only once for a spread with a model for Pix magazine. 'He wanted me to sail it and I had arranged for old Bill Anderson to buy it for me,' Heffernan said. 'But Norm (Wright) turned up with a court order for the Venom. Bob said, 'Oh bugger him, it's my boat anyway'. I didn't want to fight over it and they needed a good boat up there so I finished up going to Brisbane and buying the Taipan. Kevin Martin, a good skipper, got the Venom. Colin Clarke bought it for him.

'That year we sailed the Australian championship in Cairns. I had put new sails on the Taipan and we won easily from Venom. Kevvie said, 'Oh they sold you the wrong boat.' I said, 'Do you want to swap?' He said, 'No'. The Venom was a very good boat. Bob had fixed up all the faults from the Taipan. Unfortunately, it got wrecked up there and finished up as an oyster punt – Joey Elms had it on Moreton Bay – and they burned it, which was a pity as it would have been a good boat to keep. They have the Taipan in the Australian Maritime Museum. Jack Hamilton and I went over and identified it because they had it down as the Venom and we knew it was not.'

After Taipan, which he had re-named Crystal Lad, Heffernan quit his engineering business to spend nearly 12 months building six boats to the Taipan/Venom three-hander theme and get the new style of boat going in Sydney. They were cold-moulded with two skins of cedar angled at about 45 degrees. They had a plywood floor and unlike the hard-chined Taipan, they were round-bilged, mainly for appearance. Heffernan explains: 'Bob didn't make any attempt to make his boats look like an 18-footer. I wanted to bring them in gradually and made them look like the 18s people were used to seeing.'

With one of them, Aberdare, Heffernan won the Australian championship at Sydney in the 1962-63 season and again on the Brisbane River in 1963-64. Ken Beashel in another, Schemer, won the J.J.Giltinan series at Auckland in 1963 – comfortably in mainly fresh breezes. The boat could have won all five heats but was run down and capsized by a media launch in race three (Beashel took retribution by climbing on board and flattening the driver) and was caught out by wind shift to finish second in the last race. Bobby Holmes subsequently won the first of his five Australian championships with Schemer on Sydney Harbour in the 1964-65 season.

The move to the smaller boats and smaller crews was inevitable but traumatic at the time and many strong supporters of the 18s were lost by it forever. Heffernan reflects: 'It was a lot of trouble and good friends became bad friends. What I didn't realise at the time, the backbone of your club are not the scratch skippers; they're usually the longer markers who support all the turnouts. And we lost a lot of them over it ... who had no chance of sailing the three-handers.

'All I wanted was to be competitive with the other states and New Zealand. In a lot of ways, it was sad it happened but it was only putting off the inevitable.'

# 4

# BACK TO SYDNEY

B OB MILLER, AGED 25, RETURNED to Sydney in 1961 and for a
while worked with sailmaker Joe Pearce whose loft was busy making sails for Sir Frank Packer's America's Cup challenger Gretel. Before
leaving Brisbane, he had teamed with Craig Whitworth as crew on the
Flying Dutchman A.S.Huybers. The Queensland Yachting Association
offered the boat to Whitworth after Norm Wright was beaten in the
1960 Olympic trials on Port Phillip and lost interest in FDs. Whitworth,
crewed by John Belcher, finished second in the Australian championship to John Muston of Sydney.

The taller, heavier, Miller was better suited to the trapeze hand's role
and he had confidence in Whitworth's skippering abilities. Whitworth
had been very successful in the Gwen 12 dinghy class with Miller sails,
positioned to win the Australian championship in 1960 but lost on a
protest and finished third to Terry Gaunt's WA crew. Whitworth was a
logical thinker and good at preparing boats and campaigns. 'I was mak-

ing his sails for him and we got to be good friends,' Miller told me in the early 1970s when Miller & Whitworth were adding a yacht design section to their successful sail loft and yacht-fittings retail business in Sydney. 'He was an enthusiastic sailor and super smart. He never sailed until he was 18 but sure caught up pretty fast when he did,' said Miller.

They worked hard on the German-built FD; a beautifully-built but somewhat impractical boat, without the by then customary false floor to drain the water out; alright for the European lakes but not suited to Australian open waters like Moreton and Port Phillip Bays. 'It was a bit run down when we got it,' Miller said. 'We worked on it like a vintage car, the whole winter. We put a new rig on it, made light blocks you couldn't buy and made everything on the boat ourselves. In 1961 after we won the Australian championship on Sydney Harbour and the first Interdominion Flying Dutchman championship, also held on the harbour, we decided to stay in Sydney and open up a sailmaking business.'

Whitworth, who had been working as a salesman for his father's manufacturing business, recalled: 'We were at the presentation of trophies at the Royal Sydney Yacht Squadron when the idea of a sailmaking partnership in Sydney first occurred to me and I had a yarn with Bob on the lawn outside. 'He said, 'right oh' and a short time later we packed up our Volkswagens and headed for Sydney with no idea of where or how we were going to start and only a couple of hundred dollars between us.'

Bob Miller and Craig Whitworth unrigging the A.S.Huybers at the Royal Sydney Yacht Squadron pontoon during their successful 1961–62 FD class campaign
WHITWORTHS ARCHIVE

Craig and Bob hand-finishing sails at the Spit Junction premises
WHITWORTHS ARCHIVE

Miller had returned to Brisbane to marry Dorothy, a girl he had met there and they settled in a very contemporary house at Naraweena, a hill top suburb behind the northern beaches of Sydney.

Miller and Whitworth first set up their sailmaking business in a house Sam Weller, Alysoun Ryves' father, had bought but could not occupy as he had still to sell his previous house. Then they found an old dance hall in Military Road, Spit Junction. 'They wanted 20 dollars a week rent,' Whitworth said. 'It was more than we could afford and the hall was miles bigger than we wanted. But we saw the landlord and offered him half price. He gave it to us and we were in business.'

Craig and Bob after winning the 1967 FD Interdominion on Botany Bay with Paprika with Carl Ryves and Dick Sargeant (crew) second. From left: Carl, Craig and Dick with Bob at the back
WHITWORTHS ARCHIVE

Whitworth attended to business and added a yacht-fittings department to the loft while Miller made sails. They did not sail much for two years while they established the business. When they resumed serious sailing together, in new Flying Dutchmen called Paprika and Whittler (when he left Brisbane, Whitworth had to return A.S.Huybers to

Above: Craig and Bob on their way to winning the Australian Flying Dutchman championship on Moreton Bay, Brisbane, 1966
WHITWORTHS ARCHIVE

the Queensland Yachting Association) they quickly became the most successful Flying Dutchman crew in the country. They won the Australian championship twice and the interdominion once more.

They were an ideal combination: Whitworth was a cool, calculating

Paprika winning the Australian FD championship on the Swan River, Perth, February 1967 / WHITWORTHS ARCHIVE

helmsman who left nothing to chance in preparing a boat and had an all-consuming desire to win. Miller, the natural sailor, was an ideal trapeze man; lithe and as agile as a cat on the gunwale, ever-moving restlessly to keep the boat on her best sailing lines and lightning fast in sheeting home the big overlapping genoa through a tack and in handling the spinnaker. He was also a very talented sailmaker and innovator in rigging and fittings. With aircraft builder de Havilland, they developed a very thin aluminium mast, which proved successful while most FDs were still using hand-crafted wooden masts. They began selling them and soon spar making became another aspect of their fast-growing business.

By 1965, the sailmaking business was extremely successful with the strongest grip on the dinghy and one-design keelboat market in Sydney while Joe Pearce and Peter Cole shared the big yacht market. Miller was constantly experimenting and produced some innovative sails with venturi flaps in them to help airflow; from a venturied 'gollywobbler' for the offshore racer Ada to a Moth sail for Rick LePlastrier.

Miller was also still toying with yacht and dinghy designs. Len Heffernan, who was building his three-handed 18s at Cremorne when Miller & Whitworth started up at Mosman, remembered Miller using his shed to build a 16ft skiff with the aim of selling more skiff sails. 'I thoroughly enjoyed his company,' Heffernan said. 'He couldn't keep still ... walking up and down, telling jokes ... he was fairly entertaining. He had theories on everything. He knew a lot of things; he knew all about glider wings; he would draw aerofoil sections on the walls; he was a very interesting man.'

HE WAS IMPRACTICAL, too, at times. The skiff designed to be sailed by two was too small to be competitive in the strong 16s fleet. Miller and Ryves raced it against the Flying Dutchman but could never get it going fast enough so did not race it. Miller sold it to Lawson Abbott, a top 14-footer sailor from Manly, who won a race or two in light air but it was never successful as an all-rounder. Miller later designed successful 16s.

By then, Miller was also interested in offshore yacht design, including those within the level-rating parameters of the International Offshore Rule – particularly the One Tonners, Half Tonners and Quarter Tonners. Heffernan recalls: 'He was there at the shed one day and he said, 'they're building these Quarter Tonners wrong; they should be like this'. He drew a datum line down the wall of the shed and then the sections. 'That's how they should be,' he said. 'A year or two later a chap came down to see me, looked at the drawing on the wall and said, 'What's that there?'

'I said, 'Bobby Miller drew what he thought was what a Quarter Tonner should be like'.

'If I take this sheet of fibro can I replace it?'

'I said, 'Yeah, help yourself'. I believe he built a boat off it, from the free-hand drawing. Bob was a very good drawer'.

In 1965, Miller teamed up again with his former Star class skipper Ted Kaufman to design the very successful 42ft offshore yacht Mercedes III. They were to argue forever over who did what in the design process. Kaufman had very firm ideas about how the profile and waterline of the boat should look and that part of the boat was certainly his. He also designed the accommodation.

Mercedes III, a 1965 flier / ROSS

Miller drew the lines plans, designed the keel, worked out the lead ballast distribution and drew the sail plan which Kaufman modified slightly. Carl Ryves recalls helping Miller loft out the lines plan full size on the floor of Fairland Hall, in Hunters Hill. 'He was fiddling around with the lines full size,' said Ryves. 'The final shape happened then. We took a table of offsets of those lines.'

Mercedes III was probably the first yacht built in Australia using the cold-moulded wooden construction method, already established in building Flying Dutchmen and other dinghies. Cec Quilkey of Taren Point, renowned for building power cruisers using the cold-moulded timber method, had also built Flying Dutchmen. He constructed Mercedes III with four laminates of edge-grained Oregon, glued and fastened with Monel staples (40,000 of them per skin), over a male mould. She was light, strong, beautifully built and still racing after various owners in 1995.

Miller said the design had the profile of a Swanson boat (Ron Swanson designed a string of successful offshore racers around that time) because he could not go too far away from what Ted Kaufman wanted. 'But the beautiful thing about Ted's boat is its keel; it's a bit big but it's beautifully streamlined and that was my bit, the bloody keel. It was the most important thing.'

This was before spade rudders, separated from the keel, became the norm again in yacht design. Mercedes had a keel-hung rudder, but Miller gave it a sharp trailing edge, like a skiff or dinghy's fin, instead of just rounding it off as most other designers did at that time. The propeller aperture, between the keel and the rudder, was very tight and the keel beautifully shaped.

Mercedes III was a flier. She won nine of her first 14 races and four of the five evaluation races to gain a place in the Australian team to contest the Admiral's Cup international offshore teams' championship at Cowes, England, in 1967. The team, comprised Mercedes III, Sir Robert Crichton-Brown's Peter Nicholson-designed 46-footer Balandra and the 16-year-old Robert Clark-designed Caprice of Huon, chartered by Gordon Reynolds from owner Gordon Ingate who was tied up by the 1967 America's Cup trials between Gretel and Dame Pattie off Sydney. Australia won the Admiral's Cup by 104 points from Great Britain. Mercedes III was the top-scoring individual boat. She finished first in her class and third overall on handicap in the two long-distance and highest-scoring races of the series, the Channel race and the 605n mile Fastnet race.

Quilkey built a mark two version of the Kaufman/Miller Mercedes III design, Koomooloo, for Sydney sailor Denis O'Neil from the same frames spaced farther apart to produce a hull that was a foot longer but with the same lines. Koomooloo won the 1968 Sydney-Hobart race and a place in the 1969 Admiral's Cup team. She also represented Australia in the 1971 Admiral's Cup under her second owner, Norman Rydge Jr.

Meantime, I was on hand in Sydney to witness a notable Miller failure – structural, not design – with an Admiral's Cupper. I arrived in Sydney from a newspaper job in Melbourne in the spring of 1965 to become the first editor of Modern Boating magazine, founded by Olympic Finn sailor Colin Ryrie and Jules Feldman of Modern Magazines. A great, popular early series of features for us was the development of a method of building cruising yachts cheaply in ferro cement. The series on ferro-cement boat-building, by its New Zealand pioneer Morley Sutherland drew a huge reader response and soon amateur boatbuilders all over

Koomooloo, Mercedes III's successor, won the 1968 Sydney–Hobart race / ROSS

Australia were applying chicken mesh skins over frame-skeletons of water pipe, then impregnating the skins with a mortar of cement mixed with fly ash to improve the workability of the mix. Some were successfully completed; many others were abandoned as the dreamers realised the task was much more difficult and laborious than the Modern Boating articles had led them to believe.

Bob Miller and his friends were among the latter group. By then, I had been thoroughly captivated by Miller's free-thinking approach to boats, sailing and life in general. I'd first met him on a beach at Melbourne during a regatta. He was waving his arms and expounding ideas about a rapid succession of topics. So, when he told me about his plans to build a 35ft ferro-cement Admiral's Cupper, like his friends, I was soon absorbed by the project.

Miller enlisted as crew and co-builder his close friend Carl Ryves, Dick Sargeant and Pod O'Donnell, who had crewed for Bill Northam in his gold medal win in the 5.5 metre class at the 1964 Olympics and Bob Bull, an experienced ocean yachtsman who would be the navigator.

I duly chronicled the project in Modern Boating, under the heading 'A Cement Skimmer' as fulfilling Miller's yearning to apply his dinghy-design theories to offshore yachts and wrote: 'He has made a careful study of concrete construction from the references available in Australia and from New Zealand experience. The method of construction he is using is much lighter than that advocated by Morley Sutherland and in the meantime at least, should be classed as experimental.

'Bob's faith is strong and he is entering the boat in next season's Admiral's Cup trials. The new boat is 35ft overall, 9ft 4in beam, 6ft draft and 31ft on the waterline. She will carry a high-aspect masthead sloop rig. She is very shallow, not unlike a modern centreboarder such as the FD in profile, with small overhangs and will carry a streamlined fin-bulb keel and high-aspect ratio spade rudder.'

Miller told me: 'We have hopes that she will plane on a heavy day; not just surge, but get up and pass the waves. She has less wetted area to sail area ratio than any other yacht around and light-weather performance should be good. We have achieved this by making, theoretically at least, a more efficient fin and rudder set-up. I think concrete for this size boat has the right stiffness and right inertia for its weight. Maintenance is as low as fibreglass and fittings are easy to fasten.'

The syndicate worked hard for weeks on the ferro flier, but they were never to sail her. Carl Ryves explains why:

*IN OUR YOUNG and exuberant way, we thought we were the greatest and the ocean racing people weren't that fast. Benny always had a dream of designing an Admiral's Cup boat but none of us had any money. We formed the Whaler syndicate. I think we all put in 50 quid, which was the last we saw of it. We wanted to build a minimum-sized Admiral's Cup boat. In those days, all the yachts had rudders on the back of the keel and lots of accommodation; very much cruising type boats.*

*Benny drew up this boat which was very lightweight, looked like a canoe almost. It had very little bow and stern overhang and was quite narrow. It had a fin keel with a lead torpedo on the bottom and a separate rudder out the back. It was not unlike the old (Alan Payne-designed, 1952 Sydney-Hobart race line honours winner) Nocturne which Bob Bull had owned.*

*We wanted to build it in timber, which we couldn't afford. Benny had met this professor who said we should build it in concrete. At the time concrete boat building was very popular. Now we had a means of building this fantastic boat for very little money. Tom Mulhern, an old friend of mine – an older person who owned a lot of factories around Sydney – agreed to lend Benny and me this factory, we told him for six weeks, in the middle of Balmain.*

*We set to work, bought steel, bent it, chicken-wired it and ripped our hands to pieces. We all looked as though we had been fighting tigers. The framework didn't take too long; about six weeks. Then we tried to cement render it and had a very difficult day. We had various mates come to help us – the plan was to render the whole boat in one day. It was only going to be half an inch thick. By the end of the day we had done about 10 feet. It was thicker than half an inch and it looked terrible. So, we made the decision to unroll the fire hose and blast it all off.*

*We got 40 Italians to come in a couple of weeks later and they rendered the boat for us. But the trouble was it was now an average inch thick. It was looking way overweight but Benny, with his incredible enthusiasm, convinced us that it wouldn't matter much anyway – it was going to be so much faster than anything else although it looked twice as heavy. We were getting a bit cynical at this stage. It had a big round, rolled-over gunwale, like Venom. We were going to fit timber deck beams and a plywood deck, bolted through the concrete.*

*Weeks went by until one day, being the wood-working person in the team, I was putting in the deck beams and somehow or other dropped a G-clamp. It knocked a little hole in the bottom of the boat below where I was. But Dick Sargeant was underneath the boat and a lump of concrete as big as your head dropped off near him. So, we had a quick site meeting.*

*Sarge put his coat on and went home without saying a word. And that was the end of the concrete boat.*

*But we were stuck with this thing weighing four tons or something sitting in Tommy's factory. Benny gave the boat to Jon Mitchell, the subsequent owner of one of his Solings, who agreed to transport it out of the factory. Jon covered it with fibreglass but gave up. Then he gave it to someone else and the last time I saw it, it was being used as a houseboat in Rushcutters Bay.*

RYVES RETURNED TO racing FDs in the 1965-66 season after four years crewing with Norman Booth, his boss in a Mosman car dealership, on Dragons and 5.5 metres, and Peter (Pod) O'Donnell who was Booth's son-in-law. They sailed in a number of European regattas and that campaigning gave Ryves, who at the age of 19 had finished third to world champion Rolly Tasker and Noel Brooke in the 1960 Olympic trials, invaluable international experience.

Joining him as crew was Dick Sargeant, also working for Norm Booth. Sargeant had sailed on Gretel in the 1962 America's Cup and many ocean racing miles as well as crewing on Bill Northam's gold medal-winning 5.5 Barrenjoey. He had never sailed a dinghy before but quickly fell into the skilled ways of crewing an FD. 'He's a complete yachtsman, a great assistant ashore and all-around the course with his knowledge of sail trim, tactics and tuning,' Ryves said.

Together they built a new Sidewinder, outfitted her with Miller & Whitworth sails and spars and battled Whitworth and Miller for supremacy in the class in Sydney for the next two seasons. The fleet was strong, with up to 25 boats sailing on Botany Bay which was to be the Olympic trials venue. 'We had a lot of close racing with Craig and Bob; hardly anyone else won a race,' says Ryves. 'We used to call ourselves the works team.'

One of their notable FD opponents was Jim (now Sir James) Hardy who, crewed by Max Whitnall and using Miller & Whitworth sails won the world 505 class championship in Adelaide from Danish Olympic gold medallist Paul Elvstrøm, crewed by Pip Pearson.

A big team of more than 15 Australian boats were shipped across the Tasman for the 1966 FD interdominion on Auckland's Hauraki Gulf. Consistent Sydney crew Howard De Torres and John Pollock won sailing Kite, a new fibreglass/foam sandwich boat from the talented young Adelaide dinghy builder David Binks. Auckland crew Geoff Smale and Ralph Roberts were second, Ryves and Sargeant third and Whitworth and Miller fourth. 'We (Whitworth/Miller, Ryves/Sargeant) stuffed the regatta up by trying to beat each other,' Ryves recalls.

On the way home occurred one of Bob Miller's many airline adventures. The 30 or so Australians – sailors, their wives and girlfriends – were checking in at Auckland airport. Alysoun Ryves was on a discounted stand-by ticket, obtained because her father was an airline pilot, and would get a seat only if there was a vacant seat.

'The plane was fully booked and it didn't look like she'd get on,' Carl Ryves said. 'And right at the last minute they said they could take her. We all walked through the gate showing our boarding passes. But they sent Benny back because he didn't have a boarding pass. He hadn't checked in because he was just talking to us all. They'd obviously given his seat on the plane to Alysoun. The last we saw of him was at the desk, jumping on his ticket because they wouldn't let him on the plane. When we got to Sydney airport Dorothy, his ever-loving wife, was there. Benny didn't get home until next day.'

For the new season, Whitworth and Miller replaced their cold-moulded plywood Whittler, built by Mouldcraft, with Paprika, a new

Binks foam-sandwich hull – same construction as the Interdominion winner Kite. They won the Australian championship in Perth and so gained sponsorship from the Australian Flying Dutchman Association to go to the 1967 world championship at Montreal, Canada. At Easter, 1967, on Botany Bay, they won the Interdominion FD championship for the second time in a fleet of 51, with four wins and two seconds from Sidewinder. The 1964 Olympic gold medallists, New Zealanders Helmar Pedersen and Jack Hansen were third.

Miller, Whitworth and Ryves later in 1967 set off for Europe on a multi-purpose expedition. Whitworth and Miller were to contest the world 505 championship at La Baule, France, in August and then go on to Canada to sail Paprika in the FD worlds. Ryves was to remain at La Baule to sail a dinghy designed by Miller and called Contender in the International Yacht Racing Union evaluation trials to select a new international monotype class.

The 505 and FD campaigns of the expedition both ended in mid-fleet obscurity, but the single-hander showed promise. The IYRU trials were inconclusive. The wind failed to blow harder than 12 knots and the judges decided that more trials should be held the following year. The great English yachting writer Jack Knights, who was to become firm friends with Miller, reported: 'The Australian Contender was easily the fastest when it blew hard enough for her agile skipper to use his whole trapeze. In light airs, she usually finished in the middle of the fleet.'

Miller and Ryves had, among their many offbeat sailing projects, been sailing a pair of narrow dinghies designed by Miller, influenced by the International 10sq m Canoe, on the Lane Cove River. 'They were very narrow, probably only 3ft wide, and had an arced bottom. They were so narrow they were difficult to sail with a main and a jib,' Ryves recalls. 'On the puffy Lane Cove River they were a bit of a disaster.'

But then they heard that the IYRU was thinking about a new single-hander and that an International Canoe had starred in preliminary trials. Miller talked Craig Whitworth into supporting the project and began building a boat on the verandah of his home for the 1967 trials. Yachting journalist Lou d'Alpuget, a great friend of Miller's and somewhat a father figure, organised sponsorship for the IYRU trials campaign from Silk and Textile Printers which had been developing Contender sailcloth for the Australian America's Cup challenge. The New York Yacht Club at that time did not permit challengers to use sails made from cloth woven in the USA.

MILLER'S EXPERIENCES SAILING forward 'on the wire' in the Flying Dutchmen cemented the belief that the single-hander had to be trapeze powered. 'I tried for a boat with the highest possible power-weight ratio,' he said, 'Something like a one-man rowing shell and very fast. I also believed that it should be pretty small so that it would be easy to handle on the beach. It should be hard to sail but it should not tax the sailor to sail well.'

The first boat, built in plywood, was hard-chine, 16ft 1in long and with its 4ft 5in maximum beam well aft. The helmsman swung from his trapeze towards the stern from the heavily-raked mast. The hull cost $100 to build, the Moth-section mast and its rigging about $120, sail $90. The first boat proved very fast, planing to windward in fresh breezes, but a little difficult to manage downwind and slightly sluggish in light weather. It was also very 'boxy' in appearance. So, Miller built a second boat for La Baule with a rounded cedar chine, 4in wide at the transom tapering to one and a-half inches forward. The bottom was 3/16in plywood, topsides and deck 1/8in plywood, reinforced where the helmsman sits.

For the second set of trials, at Medemblik in Holland a year later, Miller built another boat with about two and a-half inches more freeboard. He, Whitworth and Ryves believed the Europeans were concerned about the low freeboard of the first triallist. This Contender was also slightly finer

and higher in the bow and easier to sail in light winds with end-boom sheeting and a forward well in the cockpit to take the helmsman's legs.

Steered by Craig Whitworth in the week-long trials, Contender won eight of the 16 races, including the last four. A five-man jury voted for Contender over 12 European rivals and recommended that the boat, if adopted as an international class by the IYRU, should even-

Above and opposite: Miller sailing
Skippy, the first Contender / ROSS

tually replace the Finn as the Olympic singlehander. Whitworth said the IYRU had unofficially stated that the new boat would serve for probably 20 years as an international class and be used for three Olympic Games. Miller & Whitworth began having moulds made for fibreglass manufacture. The class gained international status later in 1968.

But such are the politics of the IYRU (later known as the International Sailing Federation, and now World Sailing) the Contender is still a successful international class but has yet to gain Olympic selection while the boat it was to replace, the Finn, designed in 1949 and first used in the Olympics in 1952, is still there.

Meantime, another singlehander, the Laser, was introduced to the Olympics. Back in 1967, the Laser's designer Bruce Kirby, then editing One Design and Offshore Yachtsman magazine, visited Sydney to cover the America's Cup trials between Dame Pattie and Gretel. During the visit Ryves and Miller took him sailing on the mark II Contender on Middle Harbour. Kirby told me afterwards that he had been going to enter a boat in the La Baule trials but after he saw the Contender did not proceed because he felt he would have no hope with the boat he had contemplated. Perhaps the Contender influenced him in the subsequent Laser design, a much simpler boat without the complexity of the trapeze.

The Contender continued to attract a dedicated following of enthusiasts rising to its physical as well as tuning challenge, but not the great numbers of the Laser. Miller spoke prophetically in 1970: 'But it's a great shame, that thing. Although, and I am probably wrong here, it would have been a better boat if it had been slower, with more deadrise and deeper so you could put a single bottom in it, because it would have been better in light weather.

'But it wouldn't have won the trials Craig sailed in and it wouldn't have been been picked. It's a bit wrong the way they run those design contests. Now it goes so bloody fast on a run, it's hard to sail which may limit its initial popularity. I keep telling myself the FD would have been better if it had been slower. But the first few Flying Dutchmen ... all you used to see were upside down FDs all over the harbour but now they never capsize.

'I went out in the Australian (Contender) championship cold. The first day it blew I capsized eight times but the fellows around me didn't capsize too much and they get up that quick. It's technique and I got the technique after a while. The second day it blew, I never capsized. But a run on a heavy day will always be a frightening experience.'

Meantime, in Flying Dutchman racing through the 1967-68 summer, Ryves and Sargeant in Sidewinder gained the edge over Whitworth and Miller's Paprika. Sidewinder won the New South Wales championship, after some tremendously close racing, with 11.4 points to Paprika's 11.7. Ryves and Sargeant, who then weighed only 11 and a-half stone each, won the Australian championship and then the Olympic trials on Botany Bay, under strong pressure at the end of the regatta from Jim Hardy and Max Whitnall in Shiraz II. Whitworth and Miller's Paprika was fourth, behind Kite (Howard De Torres/John Pollock).

Ryves and Sargeant finished fourth in the Olympics at Acapulco, only .7 of a point away from the bronze medal. They felt their downwind technique let them down – important on the long ocean swells.

Miller went to Acapulco as sailmaker, maintenance man and reserve – a late addition to the team because of the Australian Olympic Committee's strict limitation of its numbers. He camped at the hotel, which served as the Olympic village, in Ryves' and Sergeant's room, sleeping on the couch as he had done at the Ryves family home and occasionally borrowing their clothes. He was valuable ashore and afloat, especially sailing as training partner for Ron Jenyns in the Finn class. He was also entertaining.

Miller sailing Skippy, the first Contender / ROSS

The Australian team was celebrating after the presentation at the end of the regatta with a party at their hotel. Paul Henderson, the Canadian Finn sailor who in the 1990s was to become president of the International Sailing Federation, had become a firm friend with Miller, takes up the story:

*THERE WAS THIS incredible party going on in the Australian room – it was a regular hotel room, pretty good size. There had to be 100 people in it; there had to be beer about an inch thick. There were feathers all over the place.*

*Ben/Bob said, 'This party is starting to drag. Henderson we're going.' So we go out and get into Ben/Bob's jeep and go down to the Whisky A-Go-Go in the middle of Acapulco. Ben/Bob goes in and hires the mariachi band, puts them in the back of the jeep with all the brass; up to the hotel, into the Australian room and demanded that this mariachi band play. With that, the police came and kicked them out.*

*Ben said, 'I don't like this place, I'm going to see Melges (the great US Olympic sailor Bob Miller had met through his Flying Dutchman campaigning)'.*

*I said, 'Melges is in Zenda, Wisconsin, Bob.'*

*'I don't care, I'm going to see Melges, I don't like this place.'*

*So off he went. You know how he used to dress, with baggy pants and floral everything he'd bought from the local goodwill store. And off we go to the airport, at kind of 11 o'clock at night.*

*So he walks up to little girl at the desk and says, 'I want a ticket on an airplane.'*

*She says, 'Where?'*

*He says, 'I didn't ask that question, I just want a ticket to get out of here.'*

*I don't know where the hell he went. But I get back home to Toronto and thought I'd better phone up my friend Melges.*

*I said, 'Buddy, by any chance has Bob shown up yet?'*

*'Oh yeah, do you want to talk to him?'*

*He had flown just in his sandals, funny shorts and coloured shirt from Acapulco to Caracas, Venezuela, from Caracas to Dallas, from Dallas to Chicago to see Buddy, because they wouldn't let his mariachi band play in the Australian room.*

After returning to Australia, Miller gave up sailing with Whitworth and moved onto a campaign in partnership with Ken Berkeley in the newly-introduced three-handed Soling keelboat class in the 1968-69 season. Whitworth, crewed by Max Whitnall, won another Flying Dutchman Australian championship with a new boat, Invader, at Hold-fast Bay, Adelaide. Miller explained: 'I'd decided to sail my own boat again. I'd had enough of being crew and I was starting to go crook, too. I was a lousy crew and I started telling the captain how to sail the boat. You get frustrated and when you start doing that, it's time to sail one yourself again.'

[Bob Miller wrote off the Mark II Contender, which Carl Ryves sailed at the La Baule trials, in a road smash on the way home to Sydney in 1968 from the Black Rock Icicle regatta in Melbourne. He escaped injury.]

# 5

# SOLING CAMPAIGN

DENIS O'NEIL JOINED BOB MILLER and Ken Berkeley in campaigning a Soling towards the 1972 Olympics. Although they were a disparate mixture of character, background and temperament they clicked as a crew. They won both the Australian championship and the pre-Olympic trials in the 1970-71 season and the Olympic trials in the 1971-72 season, sailing Berkeley's Caliph. These were significant achievements at a time when the Soling was Australia's strongest keelboat class with championship fleets of up to 70 boats, with many Australian and world champions steering them.

English-born Ken Berkeley and his brother had established a large and successful contract cleaning business in Sydney. Ken Berkeley, who was a pioneer of offshore multihull sailing in Australia, got to know Miller through being a customer for Miller & Whitworth sails. 'When I first met Ben/Bob, at his sail loft in Military Road, I was sailing big boats. He said, 'Everybody sailing big boats is an ignorant arsehole of a megalomaniac.' It's not nice being abused when you are doing your best, so I thought I had better get used to sailing little boats. At the time, Benny was sailing some-one else's Soling and couldn't stand the owner. He suggested I buy a Soling, we would get another crew and sail together.'

The other crew was another big boat sailor, Denis O'Neil, owner of Koomooloo, a development of Mercedes III, which had sailed for Australia in the 1969 Admiral's Cup team. Berkeley and Miller, the extroverts of the team, sometimes clashed famously while O'Neil, from a successful family blue-metal supplying business, was quiet and renowned for never saying a harsh word about anybody. If O'Neil really disliked someone, he would simply refer to him as, 'that unfortunate fellow'.

When Miller began sailing Solings, few believed his volatile temperament would allow him to be successful through the grind of a championship series in a slower, more tactical, boat than the adrenalin-pumping Flying Dutchman. He was still struggling with the demands on patience of light weather sailing. He and his crew finished 44th in a 53-boat fleet in frustrating light airs at the world championship on Long Island sound in 1971. But in moderate to fresh winds, his ability to tune a rig and his aggressive sailing nature made him hard to beat.

At the Long Island regatta, they bought an Elvstrøm-built boat Alexia from King Constantine of Greece and had it shipped back to Australia. It proved to be faster than Caliph, their original Australian-built boat. They won the Australian championship off Palm Beach, Sydney, from a fleet that included the American gold medallist Lowell North.

By the time of the Olympic trials on Port Phillip Bay the following season, they had worked up a good crew combination. Their spinnaker handling was a lesson for most other crews. They won four races, but two poor placings left them battling for victory right until the last race, from crews headed by Rick Le Plastrier, Alex Osborne and Ken Beashel. However, they won the last heat to seal Olympic selection.

They were a heavy crew with Berkeley about 16 stone, Miller and O'Neil each 14 stone. Miller did not feel that slowed them down in light air. 'But we're a bit awkward moving around the boat,' he said. 'We're not fairies and tend to be a bit ham fisted.'

Why did they go so well in fresh breeze? 'The weight of the crew helps. The sails are very good in fresh winds. We used yarn-tempered cloth, which doesn't stretch. The sails tend to be very flat anyway. And I know how to make a boat go in strong winds I sail the boat better in strong winds than most people do. I don't just sit there and hang out;

Above: Soling Alexia, 1972 Olympic trials
Below: Sailing Caliph in the 1972 Australian
championship / MODERN BOATING

I steer through the waves, I consider all the forces at work. I know how to trim sails for heavy weather and always have.'

Berkeley recalls that Miller could not verbalise how he sailed but when he was really concentrating, he had a method of breathing loudly through his nose. 'When he was like that, no-one could beat him,' Berkeley said. 'It was fascinating, but for some reason, I don't think he could switch it on. It happened sometimes.'

And Berkeley said Miller certainly did consider all the forces at work. 'We were off Barrenjoey (on the Palm Beach Circle course), in big waves, when suddenly he punched the boat head to wind, explaining later: 'We were going to take off and if we are in mid-air, we might as well go straight to windward.'

Miller conceded that he did not know how to trim well for light weather. 'In heavy weather, I know the way to trim and do it. In light weather, I think I know but I'm not confident so I try too many things,' he said.

Attitude helped him through the Olympic trials. 'You can tell when you're going to go well in a series if you get in the right frame of mind and I was confident after the first few races,' he said. 'I knew I could do it and even when things were against me a couple of times, I knew I was going to end up in front at the end, because of the frame I was in.'

But at the Olympics, Miller's vulnerability in light air again told against him. The Australian crew finished 16th. Miller's American friend Buddy Melges won the gold medal with a race in hand, his worst placing a fourth. The Olympic regatta at Kiel was a topsy-turvy affair in difficult and nerve-wracking light conditions. The wind never exceeded 14 knots and two days were lost in the Dragon and Soling classes to calms. Two other Australian keelboat crews were successful, with David Forbes and John Anderson winning the gold medals in the Stars and John Cuneo, Tom Anderson and John Shaw the gold in the Dragon class.

Favourites stumbled, among them Paul Elvstrøm, the six times Danish Olympic gold medallist. After a first race seventh in the Solings, he slipped to 17th from a disastrous start, came back to win the third heat and followed that with a sixth. Then in heat five, he was disqualified on two protests for barging at the lee mark. In heat six, he was forced over the line, restarted, but was so far back he retired, packed up his boat and drove home to Copenhagen. Unknown to Elvstrøm, the race was later abandoned. Had he stayed, he would still have had the chance of a medal.

Miller told his English yachting journalist friend Jack Knights that he needed one or two more years' practice in the big fleets typically found in Europe. 'If only I could get to live here for a year, I would beat those blank blank blanks.'

Knights wrote that Miller had a most disappointing series. 'But he is the first to admit he is not a light weather sailor. He had good boat speed but both he and his crew appeared to lack concentration and couldn't pick the wind shifts well enough. But then he's got a lot on his mind with new Admiral's Cup yachts and the Twelve Metre (for Alan Bond).'

Ken Berkeley maintains that Miller's design work was not a distraction to the Olympic campaign. 'No, we didn't gel,' Berkeley says. 'We didn't get on with it.'

The friendship of Berkeley and Miller/Lexcen continued for the rest of Miller's lifetime. Berkeley bought a charter yacht business, Whitsunday Yachting World and had Lexcen design the Revolution cat-rigged ketch and built three of them for charter in Vanuatu after it achieved independence in 1980. The boats, although very easy to sail with their two unstayed masts were, Berkeley found, too narrow for charter work.

Then, he commissioned Lexcen to design him a charter boat with the largest possible space inside a 40-footer. 'I suppose ten or 12 of them were built,' Berkeley said. 'It was a wonderful, big roomy boat that still sailed very well.' They used to meet regularly, once a week when Lexcen was in Sydney, throughout the America's Cup campaigning years. 'I enjoyed his company, loved him dearly and gave him a hand when I could,' Berkeley said. 'He wasn't overjoyed as he should have been after they won the America's Cup, only because of the pressure,' Berkeley said. 'He wasn't good with pressure; he just wanted to be a larrikin. And he just happened to be lucky with some of his designs, or brilliant with some of his designs.'

# 6

# THE OFFSHORE RACERS

BOB MILLER WAS ALREADY DESIGNING offshore yachts when he was sailmaking at Norman Wright's in Brisbane, under the brand name Flo-Rite, from 1958 to 1961 and designing the 18-footers and other skiffs in his spare time. 'I did a few dinghy designs in Brisbane because of the Taipan, 14-footers and things. They weren't too bad, not wonderful,' he said. 'I was always designing yachts, although no-one was building them, when I was at Norm's; imaginary yachts.'

He had a drawing table at Miller & Whitworth's Spit Junction sail loft after he returned to Sydney and teamed in business with Craig Whitworth. There, as well as his contribution to the design of Mercedes III, he designed the Contender, International 5.5 Metre class and other small yachts including in 1965, Tampico II, a 28-footer with a separate rudder on a skeg, for Arthur McKenzie-Smith.

Volante, a 50ft lightweight fast harbour racer he designed for Auck-lander Neville Price in 1968, with the shallow Flying Dutchman hull

Above: Apollo 1978 PanAm Clipper Cup
Below: Apollo, 1973 Southern Cross Cup / ROSS

form of the successful 18-footers and built with cold-moulded laminated wooden skins, led to his first big-yacht commission, Apollo, for Alan Bond of Perth. Bond's real-estate development activities of that time got him into sailing. As part of a property deal, he acquired the 51ft Panamuna from another developer. Peter Nicol had been skippering the boat, based at Royal Perth Yacht Club and originally owned by well-known West Australian yachting identity Bill Lucas, in racing on the Swan.

Unlike the previous developer owner, who had been content to just go along for the ride, Bond was keen to learn to sail. After crewing for a while on Panamuna Bond told Nicol he wanted a new boat, not only to beat Rolly Tasker's narrow 51ft Siska, the gun boat on the river at the time, but to race in the Sydney-Hobart ocean-racing classic. 'He wanted to get there first and not wait around for a corrected time result,' Nicol recalled. 'I told him he could go for the latest Sparkman & Stephens design, but might be up against two or three similar designs or go for something unconventional,' said Nicol. 'There's this young guy in Sydney getting into design with light displacement boats.'

Bond flew Nicol to Sydney to talk to Miller who told him about Volante. Bond then agreed to send Nicol on to Auckland to see Volante, which was up on the slips with a structural problem. Nicol said she was like Aucklander Jim Davern's 1966 Sydney-Hobart line honours winner Fidelis, a slender 61ft Knud Reimers design, but more modern in hull and rig. In Auckland, Nicol went for a sail on Tom Clark's Buccaneer, the 1970 Sydney-Hobart line honours winner – a fast 73ft plywood lightweight designed by John Spencer. 'Everybody I spoke to said Volante was quick, including Tom Clark,' said Nicol. 'I went back to Perth and told Bondy, 'I think if you give this guy a go he will come up with a very fast boat. He is very modern in his thinking.''

About that time, Miller & Whitworth re-located their sailmaking and chandlery business from the former dance hall at 52A Spit Road, Spit Junction, to a new 12,000sq ft building on Old Pittwater Rd, Brookvale, where a design office was added. Bond and Nicol flew to Sydney to conclude the deal with Miller and Craig Whitworth to design Apollo, a 57-ft cutter that was to become one of Miller's most successful designs.

RATING DID NOT matter. Bond wanted maximum performance for cost. Miller concluded: 'The only way to do that was to make the boat of reasonable light displacement, but a healthy type for going to sea, with a long waterline, not much overhang, easily driven and for its size, not a lot of sail. The same boat in Sydney could have had a bigger foretriangle and perhaps a bigger mainsail. But for Perth, where there is always lots of wind, the moderate sail area seemed ideal.'

The shape of the hull was dictated by reasons of economy as well as speed. As Miller put it, in his very individual mode of expression: 'I gave her a long waterline to get speed without having to build a whole lot of boat hanging out in the air not doing anything except have the wind blow on it.'

The hull was shallow, the waterline long (48ft 3in) for her overall length (57ft 3 1/2in) displacement reasonably light at 33,000lb and she had the separate rudder on a skeg that the success of the S&S designed Intrepid in the 1967 America's Cup had restored to popularity. The sailplan was 9/10ths cutter rigged

The forward sections were very slab sided with Miller reasoning that when Apollo heeled, the wall-type topsides never reached the attitude where they were lying flat in the water, as they do on boats with very long overhangs. The sections between the front of the keel and the waterline were very U-shaped. Full sections aft of the keel acted in opposition to those forward U-sections to dampen pitch. Apollo slammed going to windward rather than pitched and although she could be uncomfortable to ride, she was always fast on the wind in moderate to fresh breezes and exceptionally fast and easily driven downwind.

H. and J. Griffin of Mona Vale built Apollo, laminating five Oregon skins over very large frames and stringers. She had steel floors. All the deck beams were dovetailed with no other fixings. The 62ft long mast was stepped on deck in a tabernacle to enable Apollo to pass under the bridges across the Swan River to reach the open sea.

Apollo, designed and built to a very tight schedule spanning just seven months, was launched just in time for the 1969 Sydney-Hobart race in which she showed her potential by finishing only 18 minutes and 42 seconds behind the 62ft British cutter Crusade owned by Sir Max Aitken, which was first to finish. Apollo was crewed by Nicol and some of his Panamuna regulars and some Sydney sailors including Miller and triple Hobart race winning skipper Tryg Halvorsen.

Apollo blew out her big spinnaker on the first night and Miller spent six hours hand-sewing it back together. She gained 20 miles on Crusade in the 30-35 knot southerly that hit the fleet off the Tasmanian coast, still doing seven and a-half to eight knots under storm trysail and staysail. Miller recalled: 'We were belting into a pretty big breeze down off Tasmania. I had never designed a boat that big before and I was worrying the keel was going to fall off. While they were looking up at the sails, I was down looking under the floorboards. Tryg steered the boat for about 14 hours with an hour's break every now and then from me and half a dozen seasick guys down below. He wasn't that young then and it was really cold. But the old Viking blood was up.'

Halvorsen said: 'A man had to get a little bit of fun. She's a delight to sail. The closest thing I can compare her with is a Twelve Metre.'

Apollo in Perth soon established herself as the fastest yacht on the Swan River and in offshore events. 'She used to fly downwind,' said Nicol. 'We'd have her off the clock time after time with a rooster tail 10ft high out the back. I remember coming back from Albany in a 20-30 knot south-easter. It was just an incredible sail, in 15-metre to 20-metre high Southern Ocean swells, 400 metres to 500 metres apart. She steered like a dart and we were surfing down these things just like a surfboard, with the spinnaker collapsing inside out.'

Under the direction of Miller, one and a-half tons of lead was taken out of Apollo's keel in Perth. 'She was a little too stiff; a very powerful boat to windward but used to hurt in light going,' said Nicol.

Bond enjoyed the camaraderie and challenges of sailing, especially ocean racing with its complete separation from a hectic business life ashore. He also saw the business network opportunities offered internationally by sailing against people like Sir Max Aitken, then head of the Beaverbrook newspapers in Great Britain and Ted Turner, the founder of the CNN television network in the USA.

He shipped Apollo to the USA for the Onion Patch Trophy series and the associated Newport-Bermuda race in June 1970 and 1972. In between, Apollo returned to Australia in time to start in the rough 1970 Sydney-Hobart race, marked by hard running conditions for the first 36 hours followed by a southerly change gusting to 60 knots. She was among the 14 yachts to retire, breaking her boom off Gabo Island and then having her rudder come adrift.

Bond shipped her to England for the 1971 Fastnet race and Cowes Week where she enjoyed some match-racing battles for line honours with Ted Turner's 68ft converted Twelve Metre American Eagle. Apollo took line honours twice and American Eagle once during their Cowes Week clashes. But American Eagle was first home in the Fastnet, beating Apollo by two hours 27 minutes and setting a new record for the 605n mile course of three days, seven hours and 12 minutes.

The 1972 Bermuda race was one of the roughest with a 45-knot gale hitting the fleet towards the finish of the 635-mile course and causing widespread damage. The constant slamming as the boat dropped off waves broke frames in Apollo's forward sections and caused the deck to lift away from its support beams. Apollo had entered the 2700-mile Voyage of Discovery race, from Newport to Bayonne in Spain, to mark the return of Columbus' ship Pinta to Europe after the discovery of the New World, which followed. The crew spent most of the 11 days in Bermuda before its start repairing the damage. The Voyage of Discovery by contrast to the Bermuda race was a light-air affair. Apollo took 21 days to reach Bayonne.

As Miller expected, Apollo was at her best in strong winds and suffered in light winds for her high wetted surface to sail area ratio and her high IOR rating told against her. But under the ownership of Jack Rooklyn of Sydney, who bought Apollo in 1972, carefully planned the management of her campaign, bought new sails and put together a very experienced crew, Apollo began winning races on corrected time in the 1973-74 season as well as remaining a strong line honours contender. She took the corrected time and line honours double in the Sydney-

Brisbane race of 1973 as well as slicing ten hours off the race record.

Rooklyn took the boat back to Cowes in 1973 to win Beta Class 1 in both the Cowes-Dinard and Fastnet races. During the 1973 Southern Cross Cup in Sydney, Apollo set a record for the 180n mile 'two islands' course (around Flinders and Bird islets) and won the race on corrected time. She also won 27 nautical mile race three of the series on corrected time.

When Rooklyn had a new Miller design, the 72ft sloop Ballyhoo, built in 1974 to campaign internationally, he retained Apollo to race in Australia while Ballyhoo was overseas. When Ballyhoo was in Australia, Rooklyn's son Warwick skippered Apollo with a keen young crew. Rooklyn sold Ballyhoo after she took line honours in the 1977 Fastnet race and resumed campaigning Apollo for a line honours win in the 1978 Sydney-Hobart race. Apollo in 1979 took line honours in the Sydney-Brisbane, Brisbane-Gladstone and Gladstone-Cairns-Port Moresby race, winning the Cairns-Port Moresby 'Coral Sea' race on corrected time as well. Apollo's wonderful run came to a sad end when she was wrecked on the coral reef off Lady Elliot Island in the 1980 Brisbane-Gladstone race.

Rooklyn commissioned a successor from Miller (by then re-named Lexcen), a new 71ft Apollo. John King completed her Lexcen design

Apollo finishing 1973 Hobart race / ROSS

while Lexcen went to the USA on Australia's 1980 America's Cup campaign. In 1982, she finished just seven seconds behind Bob Bell's Condor of Bermuda in the closest finish ever to the Hobart race. Skippered by Warwick Rooklyn, she took line honours and won the IOR maxi division on handicap in the 1985 Hobart race.

Joe Adams, later to become established as a successful designer in his own right, joined Miller as a design partner and worked with him on Apollo and other designs for about two years. He left in 1971, claiming

Ballyhoo, 1975 / ROSS

he should have been given more credit for the design of Plum Crazy, Tig Thomas' and Max Bowen's Half Tonner, which won division two in the 1971 Sydney-Hobart race soon after launching and set a record for boats under 9.5m (31ft) overall length in the 1975 Sydney-Hobart race. Craig Whitworth, whose role with Miller & Whitworth at that time was essentially office administrator, recalled: 'Joe did a lot of work on Plum Crazy; exactly how much was Joe's and how much was Bob's, I don't know. I didn't get involved. But I know Joe was very unhappy because Bob got a lot of publicity on Plum Crazy. Joe said to me, 'I designed the whole boat'.'

Tig Thomas said Miller conceived the boat's shapes while Adams did the line drawings. The designer's plate on the boat did say that it was a Miller and Adams design. 'I never met Joe until we launched the boat at Clontarf,' Thomas says.

Miller's impatience with detail once he had visualised a concept, which was to flaw some of later his designs and strain relationships of those working for him, was on show in an early 1970s interview: 'I'm always drawing profiles of boats when I'm on the

Plum Crazy / ROSS

'phone. It's not hard work; I like it. I like getting the germ of an idea and getting the thing under way. But once the detail and all the fiddly bits have to be worked out, I don't like doing that.

'Joe Adams, a terrific draftsman, is now design partner. I decide what it's going to be. So, I draw a rough profile and waterlines and a few sections I want in the boat and characteristics in dotted lines like the turn of the bilge. Then Joe starts filling in the lines and if he's got a problem, or got to go one way or the other, he always consults me. And if I see after he's done something that should be a little bit different, I tell him and he alters it.'

Adams went on to design the 72ft Helsal, radically-constructed in ferro cement for Tony Fisher, which took line honours in the 1973 Sydney-Hobart race. He had her on the drawing board in 1970, before he split from Miller, when it was listed as one of their joint designs. Adams also designed the distinctively slender Adams 10 and Adams 8 metre designs, which formed popular one design classes and a number offshore designs, later in collaboration with Graham Radford.

After Miller designed Apollo, which did not rate well under the International Offshore handicap rule, Miller said: 'The modern offshore boats are designed to rules which distort their shape and make them really bitchy downwind, with enormous weather helm on a reach. This is because the International Offshore Rule evolves around measuring the length of the boat as a function of the proportion of the beam, encouraging beamier boats. But the bigger you make the beam, the crankier the boat will be downwind.'

IN 1972, WITH Denis Phillips, who had been a draftsman for the noted Sydney designer Alan Payne, designer of the America's Cup challengers Gretel and Gretel II after a number of successful ocean-racers, Miller found it was possible to design an IOR boat with the characteristics he liked. He achieved a competitive rating with a relatively light, narrow and long hull, without resorting to excessive beam in the 50ft mast-

Apollo II 1972 Admiral's Cup trials / ROSS

head sloop Ginkgo. Scott Kaufman, who had been studying the IOR rule and was to become a designer in his own right, helped Miller trim down the rating.

Denis O'Neil, owner of the 1968 Sydney-Hobart race winner Koomooloo, which was a development of Mercedes III, encouraged his friend Gary Bogard, to take on ocean racing seriously. Bogard commissioned Ginkgo and entered the trials to select the Australian team for the 1973 Admiral's Cup; a series of races for international teams that was sailed every other year from Cowes, ending with Britain's major offshore event, the 605-mile Fastnet race.

Halvorsen, Morson and Gowland cold-moulded Ginkgo from two Oregon laminates with one of Canadian cedar sandwiched between. HMG also built a sister design, Apollo II, for Alan Bond, but in aluminium to Lloyds Register scantlings for Twelve Metres to gain experience in that medium to build the Twelve Metre

Top to bottom: Ginkgo launch.
Ginkgo launch from left Bob Miller,
Gary Bogard, Trevor Gowland
Ginkgo 1972 Admiral's Cup trials / ROSS

that Miller was designing for Alan Bond's first America's Cup challenge in 1974.

At her launching, in mid-1972, Miller said he thought Ginkgo was the best boat he had designed to that time. He could not be certain. The design was intuitive; not tank tested. 'I've tried to get a long waterline for the rating (36.3ft) and the actual waterline of 41ft (42ft if you include the transom-hung rudder) is very long. The displacement of 23,000 lb is very light for a 41ft waterline length boat,' said Miller. Ginkgo carried 12,800 lb of ballast in the lead keel.

Compared to the newest Sparkman & Stephens boats of that time, Ginkgo was deep forward of the midship section, finer in the stern sections and slacker in the bilge. The fine heavily-raked entry broadened quickly to deep, full U-sections. 'The rule dictates that,' Miller explained. 'But it has got other benefits. It gives you a lot of room around the base of the mast (all the halyards exited below deck) and stops the boat pounding at sea. It's really the quietest boat I have been on in a seaway and it performs well to windward too.'

The underbody aft was fine with the waterlines running out to a relatively fine transom. The topsides protruded beyond the transom in 'planing boards' and the rudder swung from the transom on a small skeg. Apollo II's rudder was tucked under the transom. 'I tried for a boat that will be at least equal to the others on the wind in shorter races and very fast downwind,' Miller said. 'After all, in most long ocean races you crack sheets whenever you can to gain distance, rather than point high, towards the next wind change.'

The deck layouts of both boats were quite unusual for the time. They were flush decked, without the coach house providing shelter for the crew ahead of a long cockpit aft, which had been traditional to that time.

Miller was influenced by sailing on board the 68ft American Eagle, a Bill Luders-designed Twelve Metre, converted for ocean racing by her flamboyant owner USA Southerner Ted Turner, in some of the 1971 Southern Cross Cup races. 'Sailing on American Eagle showed me that the crew can stay on deck wringing wet and provided they dress for it, it does not affect them. Once you have a little cabin to shelter behind, the crew tends to hide in the cabin and not do anything. On the Eagle, everyone on watch worked all the time. A fellow stood at the coffee grinder and trimmed the genoa or the spinnaker continuously.'

The crew on Ginkgo worked in a knee-deep cockpit just aft of the mast. From there they operated the sheet winches as well as sail control

Ginkgo deck layout / ROSS

lines. The helmsman had his own small cockpit right aft. Between the two hatches on Ginkgo was a single hatch, protected by a tiny canvas dodger, leading to the main companionway. Forward of the mast was a large hatch through which sails were handed. The mast man working the battery of halyards and lifts below deck level stood under the hatch from where he could see straight up the mast and was within easy talking distance of the trimmers in the crew cockpit.

Ginkgo's accommodation, as well as the deck layout with its crew cockpit forward, was aimed to concentrate crew weight amidships. Below decks there was communal living in a vast saloon. Two berths extended side by side directly under the crew cockpit and settee berths with pilot berths behind them were ranged either side aft in the saloon. Butting the bulkhead at the forward end of the saloon, to port was the navigator's chart table and to starboard, a big U-shaped galley. Forward of that compartment again was the compartment for the diesel auxiliary engine. Crewmen had to crawl in all fours through a 'mouse hole', through the bulkhead and to the side of the engine, to reach the forepeak's sail stowage area. The toilet was housed in a box right under the forehatch to double as a step.

1972 Ginkgo / ROSS

Apollo II had a more conventional layout with a small bubble coachhouse sheltering the helmsman's cockpit and adding headroom over the galley and navigation station which were situated aft.

The sail plan on Ginkgo's masthead rig was tall and narrow with the main boom carried as close to the deck as its blocks would allow to achieve an 'endplate' effect - stopping the airflow escaping under the foot of the mainsail. The low main boom also facilitated precise adjustment of the mainsail's angle of attack for varying wind strengths. Circling the back of the crew cockpit was an elevated radial traveller to take the main boom vang; very similar to those used on the Stars. It meant that immediately the mainsail was eased for a close reach, it was effectively vanged.

Both boats had talented crews. Miller, fresh from representing Australia in Solings at the 1972 Olympics, sailed aboard Ginkgo with owner Bogard and brought along three close sailing friends in Carl Ryves, Dick Sargeant and Pod O'Donnell. All three had sailed in the Olympics; Ryves and Sargeant in the Flying Dutchman Class (1968), Sargeant and O'Donnell in Bill Northam's 5.5 metre gold medal winning crew of 1964. Sargeant and O'Donnell also crewed aboard Australian challenger Gretel in the 1962 America's Cup. Joining them were navigator Richard Hammond, who had represented Australia at two Admiral's Cups, up and coming young designer Scott Kaufman (son of Mercedes III's owner Ted Kaufman) and Alan Norman.

Apollo II's crew, with owner Alan Bond, was Jim Hardy, David Forbes, John Anderson, John Bertrand, John Longley, Ron Packer, George War-ing and John Phillips. Hardy skippered Gretel II in the 1972 America's Cup, Forbes and Anderson won gold medals at the 1972 Olympic regatta at Kiel, Germany. Bertrand had represented Australia in the Finn class at Kiel.

Ginkgo began the season by winning the Montagu Island race and concluded the Admiral's Cup trials that followed with a win in the Admiral's Cup division within the Hobart race. Her placings in the trials were 1-2-1-1-1. Apollo II, launched later and still reaching her performance peak throughout the trials placed 3-1-2-3-2. Ginkgo and Apollo II placed third and fourth overall in the 1972 Sydney-Hobart race, behind American Eagle and Gordon Ingate's 20-year-old Robert Clark designed Caprice of Huon, both helped by a new age allowance to their handicap rating. Syd Fischer's Ragamuffin, the outstanding Sparkman & Stephens 48 which had sailed for Australia in the 1969 and 1971 Admiral's Cups, winning the Fastnet race in 1971, finished the trials in third place with 2-5-3-2-3 placings to join Ginkgo and Apollo II in the Admiral's Cup team.

The Australian team prepared strongly in Sydney, with intensive training races and crew work sessions under the direction of experienced team manager Gordon Reynolds. Team captain Syd Fischer rated the team as 'undoubtedly the best Australia has chosen for any Admiral's Cup challenge.'

Ginkgo and Apollo II finished first and second in the Cowes-Dinard race, sailed in fresh wind just before the Admiral's Cup. But the German team, just as well prepared as Australia and with new boats, won the Admiral's Cup with 830 points from Australia 779 and Great Britain 749 in the 48-boat fleet from 16 nations. The Germans' flatter sails, giving them higher pointing ability, were better suited to the softer winds and quiet seas, which prevailed for the Cup that year while the Australians fuller sails had been more suited to the peculiar sloppy seas off the New South Wales coastline.

The Australian team went into the Fastnet race, which ended the Admiral's Cup, only seven points behind Germany. Then the hottest German boat, the new Sparkman & Stephens 47 Saudade, took a gamble that paid off on the final 94-mile beat in light headwinds to the finish at Plymouth. She headed well out into the English Channel to find fresher wind than yachts working the rhumb line inshore, including the Australians, which were moving only when the tide allowed them to. She finished four hours and 33 minutes ahead of Ginkgo where Ginkgo had been one hour

Ginkgo (left) at the start of the Channel race, 1973 Admiral's Cup / ROSS

and five minutes ahead of Saudade rounding Fastnet Rock.

Saudade ended the series as top boat on the individual points score with Ginkgo fourth; a good result in the strong fleet of 48 from 16 nations, but one that reflected Miller naivety about fiddling the handicap ratings. Saudade soon after the series was sold to an American. When the US measurement authorities re-inclined her in a stability test required by the International Offshore Rule, they found her rating should have been more than a foot higher than the one she carried in the Admiral's Cup.

Miller's vision was not matched by his maths. Ginkgo and Apollo really should have had more sail area to be fully competitive in the Admiral's Cup. During a minor hassle over Ginkgo's rating, with the Royal Ocean Racing Club's measurers, querying whether the planing board extension to her topsides beyond the transom extended her length, Miller was saying: 'Let's get the whole bloody boat re-measured; I'm sure we can save a foot of rating.'

Carl Ryves recalled he and Dick Sargeant looking at all the Admiral's Cup boats tied up in the Medina River at Cowes and noting that boats like Saudade, only two feet longer had masts 20ft taller. 'What's going on?' Ryves asked Miller who replied: 'We'll probably beat them anyway.' Ryves added: 'It was a good effort on Benny's part from cold turkey. Sparkman & Stephens boats had that evolution behind them; a bit more sail and a bit more waterline.'

Going back to the very first meeting he, Miller, Sargeant and Richard

Hammond had with Gary Bogard and Denis O'Neil, Ryves said: 'We went over the design drawings and naturally, typically Benny, it was going to be longer, lighter, faster, have more sail area – anything you like compared to the others.. thinking of Ragamuffin I guess. It was all those things but the trouble was the rating was 20 per cent more than Benny said it was going to be, so it probably suffered for sail area. We were all bound up with his enthusiasm.'

On the drive to that meeting, at the home of O'Neil's parents in Sydney's eastern suburbs, Miller's enthusiasm for attractive women added another passenger. Carl Ryves was at the wheel of a large expensive car on loan from Booths, the car dealership where he was working at that time, with his wife Alysoun along for the ride and Sargeant. 'We're driving through King's Cross and there's this slashing sort with a suitcase, hitchhiking on the side of the road,' Ryves recalled. 'Benny is between marriages. 'Poor Benny,' I thought he's lonely. I stopped the car. She jumped in and said she was going to some hotel so we asked her to come to dinner with us at Denis' mother's house. While we were having our meeting, we left Alysoun and this girl talking to Mrs O'Neil, a lovely lady.' Alysoun Ryves added: 'Mrs O'Neil, showing us around the house, said to this girl, 'which one is your husband?' 'Oh, none of them,' the girl replied. 'I'm just a hitchhiker.' So, Mrs O'Neil runs around the locks up all the silver and got one of the maids to stay and watch us.'

SAILING GINKGO WELL with the volatile and impetuous Miller, depended on the calming influence of his old friends Ryves, Sargeant and O'Donnell and the ocean racing experience of navigator Richard ('Sighty') Hammond, Alan Norman and Scott Kaufman. 'At first Benny thought the ocean racing people weren't that smart,' said Ryves. 'But we needed Sighty; we never would have got anywhere without him. Alan Norman and Dick Hammond were a good stabilising influence on us young clowns.

'We had good racing with Ragamuffin and the new S&S boat Queequeg. Ginkgo won almost everything here with Bundy's Apollo II second, that summer. By that stage we had Benny well trained. Sarge decided that Benny was never allowed forward of the traveller because he caused too much mayhem. And as soon as the Brookes and Gatehouse instrument showed the breeze was under ten knots, he had to go below. We had a stack of Playboy magazines down there to keep him amused.

'Benny and I were always on the same watch – Pod and Sarge on the other watch – because I could control Benny probably better than anyone else I guess. We got on so well, except he could be such a pain in light weather. When Sarge had something organised up the front, Benny would just run up and destroy everything. So, by the time we got to England, we had him fairly well under control. Benny was really the captain of Ginkgo but once we were in the ocean, Sighty was.'

Richard Hammond was to become recognised as one of Australian ocean racing's greatest navigators. He sailed on 40 Hobart races, twice on winners and in seven Admiral's Cups, including the 1979 when Australia won. He refuted the 'young clowns' comment by Ryves. 'They weren't young clowns. That outfit – boat and crew – was the best I have ever sailed with. If you end up with two big egos on a boat, or two very good sailors who have their own ideas on how things should be done, you've got a problem. On Ginkgo, we didn't have anything like that at all. They trusted one another and I had a really good role on that boat. Whatever I said they did, from A to B.

'Benny said to me one day, 'I don't know what you are doing some of the time but while we are winning you can keep doing it.' They were just good sailors, but we had them taped. Benny was not allowed to start the boat because if he started badly, for the next five or ten minutes he would keep looking around at other boats instead of concentrating on steering. He was a dreamer and liked to sail in the ocean. Pod was put on the helm whenever the situation got tight; he could pinch up. Carl was the light weather tricky helmsman and Sarge was middle of the road. Poddy would start the boat and get us through the Heads or down the track a bit, then Benny would go for a while. And if any of them were dropping off the pace, they would change immediately.'

The Hammond/Miller relationship was severely tested during the Fastnet race when Ginkgo was thundering towards Fastnet Rock, the race's major turning point off the south-west coast of Ireland. 'We were in total fog, spinnaker up doing 15 to 18 knots absolutely flat out,' said Ryves. 'We hadn't seen anything for two days. Benny is steering the boat and we are all looking for the Fastnet Rock. Sighty is getting nervous, running around the boat with his radio direction finder.

'Benny says, 'I've just seen the flashes from the Fastnet Rock light. It's behind us and we're going away from it. None of us were convinced. Benny gets Sighty totally rattled. Benny wants one of us to take over the wheel so he can go forward and pull the spinnaker down because no one else will. He's throwing a tantrum on the wheel but can't let go because the boat will broach. We are saying, 'shut up and steer the boat. Let Sighty do his thing'. We didn't do anything and five minutes later, we almost crashed into the Fastnet Rock, so Sighty was spot on.'

Ginkgo was sold in England straight after the 1973 Admiral's Cup to Italian yachtsman Giorgio Falck who was captivated by its streamlined styling. Ken Berkeley recalled Benny's account of the transaction:

'He was on the boat when this bloke in a daggy old outfit came along and said in a broken accent, 'It's a beautiful boat'.

'Benny said, 'Would you like to have a look?'

'How much do you want for it?

'Let's say the asking price was $300,000, Benny said, '$550,000'.

'Would you keep it for two hours and I will bring the money?'

'Benny said, 'sure'.

'Two hours later, back he came in his daggy gear and behind him an associate in an immaculate suit with a duffle bag containing $550,000 in cash. The bloke in the daggy outfit owned steel mills in northern Italy.'

Falck re-named Ginkgo Guia III and raced her successfully. She was a member of the 1975 Italian Admiral's Cup team. She finished second in one race and top-scored for the Italian team. The following year, a killer whale holed her and she sank quickly while racing south-west of the Cape Verde islands in the Atlantic. The crew of six was rescued after spending 18 hours in the life raft.

Miller's reputation as a designer of offshore yachts, following the successes of Ginkgo and Apollo II, was further reinforced by having two new One Tonner designs, Ceil III and Rampage, finish first and third on corrected time in the 1973 Sydney-Hobart race. The One Tonners had long, relatively narrow and deep shapes and lightweight hulls similar in concept to Ginkgo and Apollo II. Hong Kong sailor Bill Turnbull commissioned Ceil III, which was built precisely by Sydney craftsman Doug Brooker of three laminated skins of silver silkwood. Craig Whitworth project managed the building and outfit of the boat while Dick Sargeant, manager of the M&W sail loft, joined him in rigging and tuning her. They crewed her in the Hobart race and Southern Cross Cup series of shorter races associated with the Hobart, along with other good Sydney sailors John Wigan, who navigated, Doug Patterson and Scott Kaufman.

The downwind conditions that prevailed for the 1973 Hobart race suited Ceil III's long waterline shape. The 40-footer was alongside the S&S 47 Queequeg for the first two days of the race. Ceil III was knocked flat in frightening gybe/broach while the crew was preparing to drop

Top to bottom: Ceill III launch; Ceill III; Ceill III, 1973 Hobart winner, leaving Sydney / ROSS

the spinnaker after rounding Tasman Island for the last leg to the finish. Whitworth went overboard in the wipe-out. 'The boat went over to windward,' said Whitworth. 'We got some bullets coming out into Storm Bay. I was standing by the cap shroud, just having a look, when we went over and dipped the mast in. I went overboard, grabbed a rope hanging overboard and they pulled me on board.

'The crew of a nearby boat pulled their spinnaker down and came over to help us because we'd disappeared; they thought we had gone. We came up, sails flogging, pulled them on and off we went again. Those were the days when you thought you were indestructible.'

Ceil III came up without a drop of water below, ready to race on. 'Only the eggs were broken,' said Bill Turnbull, 'She's a great boat.'

The British yacht Prospect of Whitby (Arthur Slater) was second, two hours and one minute behind Ceil III, with Rampage third, another 34 minutes behind. Rampage, owned by Dr Peter Packer of Perth, was to win the Hobart race

Ceil III crew, from left: Owner Bill Turnbull, Dick Sargeant (M&W sail loft manager), Scott Kaufman, Doug Patterson and Craig Whitworth (sailing master) relax at Constitution Dock / WHITWORTHS ARCHIVE

in 1975. She had the same hull shape and dimensions as Ceil III but carried a 4ft taller mast and more sail area which pushed her handicap rating under the International Offshore Rating rule from 27.5ft (One Ton class) to 29.9ft.

# 7

# SOUTHERN CROSS, THE SETBACK

ALAN BOND'S INTEREST IN THE America's Cup, kindled by the clash with Vic Romagna in June 1970 (chapter one), firmed through the Cup match in September that year. The US defender Intrepid, skippered by Bill Ficker, won 4-1. But the Alan Payne-designed Australian challenger Gretel II, skippered by Jim Hardy, showed great promise. Gretel II won a race and finished first in another, coming from behind after a start line collision only to lose that win on a controversial protest arising from the collision.

Bond challenged through Royal Perth YC soon after that contest, on September 29, 1970 and the following year bought Gretel and Gretel II from Sir Frank Packer when a proposed Sydney syndicate failed to eventuate. He shipped them to Fremantle in 1972 for crew training. Gretel II later was to be the pacemaker for a new International Twelve Metre class challenger to be designed by Miller. The International Yacht Racing Union meantime decided to allow aluminium construction for the new

Twelves. The decision of the New York Yacht Club to set the date for the following challenge back a year to 1974 meant the next generation of America's Cup boats could be made of aluminium and be about 15 per cent lighter. The wooden Gretel II was no longer competitive.

Bond through his overseas campaigning had seen the opportunities that sailing presented in creating business. He decided to base his America's Cup preparation on his first big property development, Yanchep Sun City. He had bought a 19,000-acre cattle property with 17km of sea front 47km north of Perth and had it re-zoned for residential development. The cocky 33-year-old gained approval for his master plan to establish an entire city on the site from the West Australian government with the argument that he was going to win the America's Cup and bring it back to put Yanchep on the map as an international sporting destination.

To stabilise the rolling coastal sand dunes of the property and make it look good in brochures and advertisements, Bond Corporation mixed green paint and grass seeds with a light bitumen to spray on the sand dunes. In the first 12 months, it sold 1350 blocks of land there. Bond Corporation built holiday houses and spent $1.25 million on developing a harbour, protected by extending breakwaters around the fishing port of Two Rocks, with a marina that was to ultimately have 550 berths.

Miller & Whitworth, a buzzing, stimulating work place through 1972-73 with spar-making added to the successful sail-loft and chandlery, added young talent to handle the extra workload of designing the America's Cup challenger. Joining Miller, then 36 and Denis Phillips (31) were John Bertrand (25), to be responsible for sail and spar development and John King (22), as a draftsman and trouble shooter for the whole project. Bertrand's sometime rocky association with Miller was to continue until 1983

Alan Bond at Yanchep, 1973

Yanchep under construction

when he finally steered Alan Bond's Australia II, designed by Miller (by then Lexcen) to win the America's Cup.

Bertrand brought science, as well as natural skill, to his sailing. He majored in aeronautics when he gained his degree in mechanical engineering from Monash University in Melbourne. His thesis was on the optimum setting of sails for Twelve Metre yachts when going to windward. So, when he joined Gretel II as a trimmer for the 1970 America's Cup challenger, Jim Hardy's crew named him 'Aero'.

He and his wife Rasa stayed in the USA after the Cup while Bertrand took up a scholarship at the Massachusetts Institute of Technology. During the 20 months he spent there completing a Master of Science degree, his friend Robbie Doyle introduced him to racing in a Finn, the Olympic single-handed dinghy. Bertrand, who had won an Australian Junior VJ championship and an Australian Lightweight Sharpie championship, soon mastered the physically demanding Finn and finished fifth in the 1971 Gold Cup world championship in Canada. That placing, the highest by an Australian to that time, encouraged him to return to Melbourne where he won the selection trials for the 1972 Australian Olympic team in the Finn class.

Miller, who won selection for the Australian team as skipper in the Soling class, soon after the trials approached Bertrand at Royal Brighton Yacht Club and asked him to consider working with him on the America's Cup design. Bertrand accepted and soon after the Olympic regatta at Kiel, Germany, where Bertrand finished fourth and Miller 16th, the Bertrands moved to Sydney. Although he was not involved in the ocean-racer designs, Bertrand sailed aboard Alan Bond's Apollo II to win selection in the Australian Admiral's Cup team and to sail on her in England.

He spent three months overseas researching sailcloth development. Experience and experiment in developing the sails for Ginkgo and Apollo II helped that research. Halvorsen, Morson and Gowland built Apollo II in aluminium to the Lloyds scantlings for Twelve Metres to gain experience in that medium for the Bond America's Cup challenger.

The Bertrands had little money after campaigning on the international Finn circuit for two years. Miller lent them one of his cars, 'his little Austin Sprite which could just get up the Spit Road hill belching smoke out the back,' Bertrand recalls. 'He would lend you his last dollar. We became very close friends.' When their first child, Lucas, was born, Miller became godfather. 'He loved Rasa; he would come around and we had lots of dinners together.'

The volatile Miller held all working at M&W enthralled as he spun out his jokes, his dreams and also vented his impatience. When things weren't going his way, he would throw chairs around, punch walls and chuck scissors and spikes across the sail loft with such frequency that all the seamstresses would automatically duck for cover. 'They would gracefully slide under their benches, like a Swan Lake ballet,' Bertrand said.

Every lunch break was a dream build; winning the America's Cup or Olympic campaigning in Europe half the year from a villa with a collection of Olympic and international class boats and a collection of old cars to tow them around. Here is Miller on that theme:

*I have a pipe dream of a sail loft in Spain where you could save enough money working at it to make it a depot for people to go and live there from Australia just to compete in European championships. I guess I'll do it one day, as soon as I can.*

*We are just always one step behind the good guys in Europe now. In the old days, you could be up with them because the Australians and New Zealanders are innovators by necessity and the Europeans weren't. They used to buy a boat and sail it as it came. We used to make all our own stuff and because you'd think about it more, you made it better. But these days they're innovators too and there are so many more of them. Their boats are technically better than ours, always.*

'We were going to conquer the world,' said Bertrand. 'The man was amazing, complex, brilliant and driven. Let's face it, he had successes and failures and that was part of his drive; just keep pushing forward and forward. And he loved that space; he loved the concept of boats driving through the water and sails going through the air.'

Miller drew his understanding of those concepts from natural sources as well as books. Bertrand remembers sitting with him on Manly beach, watching the seagulls fly in to land. 'He could see them just feeling the vortices – the turbulence coming off trailing edge of their wing feathers

– as a result feeling whether the bird is in a stalled condition or not and coming into the most perfect landings every time.'

The Miller team tank tested many shapes in the Sydney University towing tank, where models of Dame Pattie and Gretel II had been tested. The six models were altered many times and models of Intrepid and Gretel II were also towed for comparative purposes. Mast models were wind tunnel-tested and sailcloth researched. With suitable Bainbridge Vectis and Hood cloth now available from mills in Europe and the Australian-made Contender cloth suitable for headsails and spinnakers, the prohibition on the use of US-made cloth to the challengers was no longer a problem.

Because the boat was the first to be built in aluminium, Bond took extreme security measures to prevent outsiders from seeing the hull. It was shrouded in a tarpaulin, with tin-foil underneath to thwart infra-red photography on its journey from the corrugated iron shed where Halvorsen, Morson and Gowland built it in secrecy in the bush-clad outer suburb of Terrey Hills to the Sydney wharves for shipping to Fremantle.

She went on by road to Yanchep where crew-training was by now under way between Gretel and Gretel II under the supervision of Bond's nominated America's Cup skipper John Cuneo, the gold medallist in the Dragon class at the 1972 Olympics. The boat was finally prepared in a brick shed at Yanchep that alone cost $200,000 to build. A 10ft high wire fence kept outsiders away and at night guard dogs roamed the premises.

Cuneo and his potential crew were the 'Wild West' pioneers of

M&W 1973 design team, from left: John Bertrand,
John King, Bob Miller, Denis Phillips / ROSS

Yanchep, which became a popular holiday resort town of about 4,500, with two golf courses, horse and camel riding and a modern shopping complex.

When Cuneo moved there with his wife Joy and two of their four sons in September 1973, the marina was still under construction and the shed to house the Twelve was not finished. For two weeks he worked from a construction hut on the sand dunes overlooking the marina, which was still being torn out of the sand and rock by heavy earth-moving machinery. There was no telephone in the challenger's shed until late November when a special radio-telephone was installed to link it with the Bond Corporation offices in Perth and through that to the outside world. Until then, all telephone calls had to be made from a shop five miles away.

When easterly winds blew strongly from the inland, they sent the temperatures up to 33C and blasted a sandstorm across the marina from the dunes laid bare by the construction work behind it. Pesky bush flies abounded, so badly that the place became known to the sailors as Yanchep Fly City. One worker reported on a job at the marina in an apiarist's hat and veil.

The Twelve Metre crewmen were almost all employed at Yanchep, either on finishing off the new Twelve and maintaining the Gretels or on one of the many construction projects. They sailed both days each weekend in match-race training on the Gretels. By the time the new yacht was launched, they had sailed 83 match races in three months.

They lived in houses provided by the Bond Corporation. The nearest pub was ten miles away. Attending dinner parties at each other's houses was the major social activity. There were facilities for healthy living: tennis courts, a pool and the sea for swimming, horseback riding and good fishing. It was much like a boxer's training camp with few distractions. Those working on the boats had only one day off each week, Thursday.

The secrecy surrounding the new boat had the effect Bond's shrewd public relations team wanted. It generated international publicity. Photographers and reporters gathered and waited patiently in the sandhills and ti-tree scrub for the boat to first emerge from its shed in November 1973. I was among them, had a furtive meeting or two after dark with Miller and crewmen from Sydney I knew well but gained little information, apart from learning when the boat was first due to appear.

When the hull, painted yellow in keeping with the Yanchep sun theme, did finally emerge from the shed, with a hydraulic Tami lift wheeling it to the water, it was draped in a cloth skirt and a tent covered the whole deck area aft of the mast. While other photographers played hide-and-seek to get a picture as the hull slid into the water and the skirt was removed, one young photographer from a Perth daily newspaper wandered obviously out onto the breakwater opposite and began snapping away with a long lens.

Within minutes, a utility load of hefty crewmen joined him and invited him to accompany them back to the shed where John Cuneo told him he was trespassing and asked him to expose the film. The photographer obliged. While this was going on a tourist with a box camera had snapped a picture and gave the film to the photographer's opposition newspaper, which published it on the front page. The editor of the first newspaper heatedly complained to the Bond syndicate heads who then allowed official photograph to be taken from the bows of the boat in the pen, but with the after deck still covered.

When the boat, then named Australis, went sailing for the first time four days later I hitched a ride with a couple of fishermen to shadow her to get a picture. The fishermen were only too happy to help me; to them, Bond was an unwanted intruder at the Two Rocks inlet. I had already

Southern Cross off Yanchep / ROSS

undertaken not to take any photographs of the deck layout, which might assist syndicates overseas. But all the security fell apart when a newspaper photographer flew over in a light plane to get pictures published the following day on the front cover

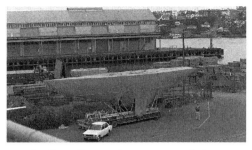

Southern Cross under wraps on a Sydney wharf on the way to WA / ROSS

and inside pages of the Sunday Times which clearly showed the deck layout. It had five waist-deep openings to keep crew weight low and reduce windage, three winch drums in line down the deck and a big rectangular helmsman's cockpit aft with twin steering wheels.

When Gretel II and Gretel joined her in that first tentative outing in a light 5-8 knot breeze that gradually increased to 12, the new boat was dramatically faster reaching and running. But upwind she was not pointing as high as Gretel II and as the sea breeze freshened was struggling to hold her off. That first sail was ominous.

Miller, with his intuition for fast shapes distorted by the tank testing results, had opted for a very long hull, about eight feet longer than Gretel II's with a long bow overhang. Above the waterline, the bow cut away in hollow to maintain a short measured waterline length but pick up effective sailing waterline length when the boat was heeled. Maintaining a shorter measured waterline allowed a sail area as big as Gretel II's within the Twelve Metre rule rating

Australis (as originally named) on an early sail / ROSS

formula. The hull was beamy with the after overhang relatively long and flat, promising speed downwind. However, the hull was relatively full forward, which was to lead to the Bond challenge's 0-4 defeat in the 1974 match to Sparkman & Stephens' newest design Courageous; a lighter, shorter, finer hull carrying more sail area.

The new boat, officially named Southern Cross at a ceremony in January, was beset by equipment problems at Yanchep. Miller's policy of using the lightest possible fittings and then replacing them with stronger ones when they broke was one factor. And many of the crew, which was charged with fitting out the boat, had not worked with metal before. Strong winds through several weekends in January kept the Twelves in port and then Southern Cross broke her mast in February.

Speed testing and racing between Southern Cross, skippered by Cuneo with John Bertrand as tactician and Gretel II, skippered by Jim Hardy did not conclusively show that the new boat was any faster than the four-year-old wooden Gretel II. Bertrand said: 'Naturally everyone wanted the new boat, Southern Cross, to be fast, really fast; a lot faster than the defeated Gretel II. And I think that subconsciously we were prepared to do almost anything to make this a reality, whether it was

Southern Cross trialling against Gretel II off Yanchep

true or not. For instance, we always put the best sails on Southern Cross and the bad ones on Gretel.'

DISSENSION WITH CUNEO'S leadership style was also growing. Cuneo, a brilliant sailor, a perfectionist, was leading his big and disparate team of individuals like a schoolmaster. 'We were supposed to be a team, but John Cuneo found it difficult to master the subtle art of making people want to work for him,' Bertrand said. So, Bertrand resigned as tactician and became mainsheet trimmer. Hugh Treharne joined the crew as tactician and Dick Sargeant as forward hand. And by the time Southern Cross and Gretel II were shipped from Fremantle to the USA in late April, Bond confirmed the conjecture of some weeks that Hardy could replace Cuneo as skipper after more trial racing at the America's Cup venue, Newport, Rhode Island, USA in early July.

Bumptious Alan Bond, then on the rising of his meteoric parabola in business, went to Newport confident that Southern Cross was going to win the America's Cup and let the conservative New York Yacht Club know that, all boastful guns blazing. His confident publicity campaign had already backfired. It encouraged the members of the defending New York Yacht Club to build two new aluminium boats, the radical Mariner designed by Britton Chance and the Sparkman & Stephens-designed Courageous, while a Seattle-based syndicate rebuilt the wooden Intrepid to her original and probably faster 1967 shape. This was to a re-design by Olin Stephens to Chance's re-design for the 1970 challenge.

While Southern Cross was easily defeating Baron Bich's France, a re-design of the boat Gretel II defeated in the 1970 challenger eliminations, 4-0 to become challenger, over on the defender course, Intrepid was giving Courageous a battle for survival. It came down to a win by Courageous on the last available day of racing after they had been tied at four wins each. This deadly struggle eliminated people as well as the boats. To break the stalemate, Bob Bavier, the skipper of Constellation in the 1964 Cup win, stepped down as skipper of Courageous and handed the helm to sailmaker Ted Hood, who went on board initially for his trimming skills. Dennis Conner, a 28-year-old Congressional Cup champion from San Diego, who had skippered the unsuccessful Mariner earlier in the defender trials, joined Hood as starting helmsman and tactician.

The announcement of Conner's appointment prompted an extraordinary response from Bond. In a prepared statement, he said: 'We are extremely apprehensive and concerned to learn of Conner's appointment specifically in the role of starting helmsman. Conner has a reputation as an aggressive helmsman in America's Cup racing and we are fearful that fouling and striking tactics will be introduced in America's Cup starts.

'These tactics are an accepted part of Congressional Cup racing but would prove extremely dangerous if used in actual America's Cup events. Conner has already been involved in three protest situations during the present US elimination series proving that his approach is one of pressure tactics along the lines of Congressional Cup racing rather than on the codes of strict sailing skills of crew and boat.

'We deplore this approach, which is degrading to the dignity and prestige of the America's Cup as one of the world's most important sporting events. We are most concerned that this style of racing could be condoned by the New York Yacht Club to seriously disadvantage our efforts. Apart from the unsportsmanlike nature of this approach, there is a definite element of danger to the safety of the crews and the boats by adoption of rodeo tactics afloat.'

Bond in his first America's Cup campaign was an interfering and sometimes irrational syndicate head. In Newport, as expected after sailing more trial races between Southern Cross and Gretel II, he replaced Cuneo with Hardy as skipper. Southern Cross beat France by huge margins: 7min 32 sec, 3min 37sec, 6min 59sec, 4min 22sec. Bond exuded confidence after Southern Cross admitted the coup de grace: 'This was a good race today in a good breeze. There seems little doubt we will win the America's Cup too.'

But Miller knew Southern Cross had to go faster to beat the US defender. In Newport he fitted her with a three-part articulated rudder blade, designed and built by Italian engineer Nino Pecorari, for improved lift and less steering effort. And after the elimination series against France, he changed the rod rigging on Southern Cross from 5/8in to 7/16in for a weight saving aloft of 45lb, about half the weight of the earlier rigging. Stresses had been carefully calculated on each component of the rig through training, back to the Yanchep days, with strain gauges connected to a computer in the cockpit. Could it break? 'It's all stops out now,' said Miller with a shrug. 'We have simply got to try everything.'

Courageous won the America's Cup match in a walkover, beating Southern Cross by margins of 4min 54sec, 1min 11sec, 5min 27sec and 7min 19sec. Tactical errors lost Jim Hardy and his crew the lead on the first beats of the first two races. Southern Cross had enough reaching speed to consolidate any first beat lead on the two reaching legs of the course that followed on the triangle-windward-return 24.3n mile America's Cup course of those days and a chance of winning by applying conventional covering tactics for the remainder of the race.

Alan Bond, who had placed himself on board for the second race as a grinder hand to 'give the crew a bit of a lift', reacted irrationally, sacking both tactician Hugh Treharne and navigator Ron Packer. He replaced Treharne with Cuneo and Packer with Jack Baxter. The Australians' morale fell away from there while Courageous, her crew gathering confidence in themselves and the boat, just went faster. She had basically more sail area pushing a finer, lighter hull through the water. All the evidence I could collect suggested that Courageous was 1700 lb lighter than Southern Cross but carrying 57sq ft more working sail area.

While Courageous, with a shallower hull depending more on the

America's Cup start

keel for lateral resistance, pitched slightly more and heeled more on the wind, she almost always could outpoint Southern Cross. There was very little difference in the aft sections. Courageous did have a trim tab on the keel while Southern Cross did not. Southern Cross may have been fractionally faster reaching, but running square, she lost ground in all but one race. She did give promise of good fresh wind ability in race two when the wind speed got up to 16 knots. The other three races were sailed in 12 knots or less with flat seas. Jim Hardy sailed Courageous the day after the defender's 4-0 clean sweep and said it was like driving a V8 after a Straight 6.

The result devastated Miller while Bond remained as ebullient as ever. At the final press conference in Newport, after generously congratulating the winners, Bond made a last grab for the headlines and publicity for Yanchep Sun City. He said he would sponsor a Twelve Metre world championship, to be sailed from Yanchep in October 1976. He would donate a gold cup valued at Aus $25,000 and offered free transport to the first three nominations. It never happened.

Bond went home regarding the loss as a lesson learned and determined to challenge again. He said in his autobiography: 'For me, the America's Cup campaign was simply an extension of the 29 companies I had in the Bond Corporation stable at the time – the challenge was as much a business as any of them and I could see a profit at the end, win or lose.'

Miller at the final press conference, in answer to a question, said Gretel II had been a good yardstick for Southern Cross but added: 'Unfortunately Olin Stephens is getting older and smarter. I hope there is not much room for him to get any smarter and for me to get smarter. But we will have another go, I think.'

A FEW DAYS later, in an interview I had with Miller at the apartment he was sharing with his wife Yvonne in Newport, he took the blame for Southern Cross' failure in a subdued mood that was later to develop into 'Black Dog' depression. I asked him why the Southern Cross hull was full in the front while the Courageous hull was finer and more veed forward. 'The [towing test] tank told me full in the front was good,' Miller said. 'I hated the tank and did not believe it but once you get down to the ground level of something like that, you cannot help but believe it. It was easier to believe. Here is a piece of paper with the performance of the boat and you don't have to rack your brains.'

[Miller's testing had been in the University of Sydney tank. Although the designs of the previous two Australian challengers Dame Pattie (1967) and Gretel II (1970) had also been tested there, the tank was smaller and by no means as sophisticated as the tanks available to the American designers. At that time, the America's Cup rules denied the challengers access to tanks outside the country of origin.]

'Olin Stephens told me after the America's Cup that he gave his tank fellows certain limits they were not to exceed. He told them, 'I don't want any less lateral plane than this and I don't want the stern to be any blunter than that, because the blunter you make it the better it shows in the tank', like Mariner and I knew that.'

Miller said he had designed Southern Cross for stronger winds than experienced in the America's Cup. 'I believed that if we could build a boat that was different to theirs, it would not matter if the crew was worse if it blew. And Courageous does tip over, 20 degrees more than anyone else (in windy conditions) and we could beat it. We have been out there and really chewed it up in heavy wind, upwind and down, particularly downwind. And it pitched a lot because it had a veed bow.

'I also expected rougher water. The perfect place to tune up a Twelve Metre is off Sydney Heads. You get the joggle from the cliffs that is a lot like spectator wash and you get a lot of sick southeast winds. The whole year at Yanchep was wasted, although looking at it from the other side of things, if there was no Yanchep, Alan Bond could not have afforded to challenge.'

Miller said he felt Bond would challenge again. 'Straight after the America's Cup I felt bad; he had spent $3 million. I went down to apologise and he said, 'Don't you worry about it. I have lost more money than that in an afternoon.' He said as far as he was concerned the boat was okay ...I might have made a mistake in the sail area, it had a six-cylinder engine instead of an eight. And he was really good about it. He has gone off smiling.'

Miller said the Americans could throw a Twelve Metre like Courageous into the water and get it up to pace in three months because they had a lot of experience in preparing for the America's Cup. 'When I arrived in Newport they were hopeless. I watched Courageous and Intrepid race and they were pretty bad. But I went back six weeks later to watch and they were polished.

'They do start out with better raw materials. We sieve the country for people who want to do it for a start and pull out those who have done something. The longer you make the program, the fewer good people you are going to get. The reason our fellows folded in the last race was because they had been at it so long. As soon as they were beaten and lost the Superman image they had built up around themselves they went down like a pack of cards; they couldn't take it. After race two it was all over. The first two races were genuine bungles. They crossed the other boat and then didn't know where the layline was ... the poor damned tactician had to decide his tactics without knowing where the layline was.

'But I don't blame those guys for what happened. I blame myself. I screwed up, not the crew. If the boat had been made a little bit faster they would not have been under pressure and made the mistakes in the first two races. I am to blame. Alan Bond practically gave me carte blanche. And at the end where people started taking control and squeezing me out – they didn't really squeeze me out but gave me such a bad time – I let them have control. It was actually my lack of confidence in myself that let them change things and do what they wanted to do.'

What sort of things went wrong? 'Things like the computer. In our dumb Australian way, we buy a really big computer – as big as a typewriter – the most sophisticated desk-top computer you can get of the type that put a man on the moon. We build an inverter to the electricity from the batteries into 110 volts so it will work. Then we have 30 batteries on the boat for power, which does not matter as they are all down in the ballast. The whole lot weighed 300 lb. And we had interfaces made to turn the input from the Brookes and Gatehouse and other electronic gadgets into language the computer could understand. The computer was not unreliable, the instruments were not very unreliable, but the interfaces that were made by an Australian were unreliable and we discarded the whole system.

'Now I go on board Courageous and find a computer nowhere near as sophisticated as ours but one that does enough to be useful. They had predicted curves for performance under different sails and we had those. The computer was supposed to tell the difference between the predicted curves and the real curves. Their computer was handmade and worked. Olin Stephens told me it was unreliable for a long time, but it worked during the series. Where it worked for them most was downwind. Now I am sure our boat was faster downwind; when the two boats were close together downwind our boat gained and when they were a long way apart our boat lost.

'If you are sailing on the wind the helmsman is more accurate than the computer because your VMG curve at different angles to the wind is a pretty tight curve. You are looking at the peak of the curve and it is easy to find that just by looking at the instruments and using your judgement. But the downwind curve is really flat and to find the peak of it is very difficult. The computer did that for Courageous.'

# 8

# MILLER AND WHITWORTH SPLIT

BOB MILLER WENT HOME FROM the crushing America's Cup defeat in September 1974 to a new Australian sailing season that was to be littered with more setbacks for his new ocean racer designs. This intensified the bouts of depression, which always alternated with his entertaining high spirits and ultimately led to the unravelling of his partnership with Craig Whitworth the following year.

The success of Ginkgo, Apollo II and Ceil III had prompted demand for M&W offshore designs in Australia and abroad through 1974. Syd Fischer and Alan Bond had new M&W 54 footers built to contest trials for the Australian team to contest the 1975 Admiral's Cup. Fischer's second Ragamuffin and Bond's Apollo III were in proportion narrower, deeper and heavier than Ginkgo and carried more sail. Apollo III had a distinct chine in her topsides aft to reduce handicap rating.

Ian Perdriau built Ragamuffin in aluminium in Fischer's own boatbuilding factory at Rozelle. Halvorsen Gowland built in aluminium both Apollo III and Ballyhoo, which was a new Miller-designed 72-footer commissioned by Jack Rooklyn, who had bought Apollo from Alan Bond. Olympic Yachts in Greece commissioned a 48ft design with streamlined styling to put into fibreglass production as the Olympic 484 for the European market. Sydney offshore sailor Geoff Lee bought the first of them, Geronimo, and had her shipped out for the Admiral's Cup trials in early 1975.

Besides the America's Cup campaign other distractions removed Miller from the day-to-day design and sailmaking work at Brookvale. He was indulging his love of fast cars with a succession of two second-hand Ferraris that kept demanding time and money on maintenance and repair. Once he picked up the Ferrari from a garage in Brookvale, where it had been having work done on the gearbox, to find that had ended up with four reverse speeds and one forward. A new keel for Apollo III was held up for a week while Miller, who was meant to be designing it, had the engine out of the red Ferrari.

His friend and partner Craig Whitworth continued to admire and encourage Miller's creative ability through this turbulent period that was eventually to end their association. Dick Sargeant, who managed the Miller & Whitworth sail loft from late 1973, said: 'I thought Craig was very tolerant of Benny. He was meant to be a partner, the creative guy, but he was never there while Craig was there every day, eight to five. At one stage, he was meant to be designing the keel for Apollo III but instead, he'd had the engine out of the Ferrari for a week.'

Whitworth recalled: 'I would be struggling with creditors and Bob would come back with a Ferrari! But I haven't got anything bad to say about him. He was just a fantastic character. I lived with it for a long time where a lot of other people would have given up, but I have always appreciated creative people and I have been very tolerant of them, I think. It was difficult in that he was an absolute loose cannon.'

Once Miller blasted across the Warringah Mall car park in his newest-acquired Ferrari and up the grass slope to park among the trees just outside Miller & Whitworth's sail loft. He jumped out, threw the door open and yelled to Whitworth, who was standing outside, 'What do you think?'

'Great!' said Whitworth.

'He hadn't put the hand brake on and it rolled backwards, caught the aluminium door in a tree and folded it back,' Whitworth said. 'So, Bob goes berserk, there was more than a couple of thousand dollars damage.'

Sail testing platform on the roof of Miller & Whitworth's Brookvale premises / WHITWORTHS ARCHIVE

I experienced first-hand Miller's snap descent into tantrum, followed by depression at reversals early in the season of 1974-75. Graham Oborn, a Finn-sailing friend, commissioned a design for a new Half Tonner to go ocean racing. Knowing I had raced offshore, Oborn invited me along on its initial racing while Miller was on board. Level rating racing – for boats sailing to a single rating number under the International Offshore Rule – was riding a surge of popularity world-wide at that time in Quarter, Half, Threequarter, One and Two Ton classes. The Half Tonners were particularly popular in Sydney with up to 20 of them racing as a class each weekend.

The first race for Hot Bubbles went well for us with a flat sea, the boat showing good speed downwind and Miller calling tactics inspirationally and being an engaging and amusing sailing companion. The next one was an emotional disaster. The day began badly when Miller's new cashmere sweater went overboard while we were still alongside the dock at the Clontarf boatshed. I jumped in the water to retrieve it as it drifted away, earning a nice pat on the head from Bob.

But later that day I was on the receiving end of a classic Miller tantrum along with the rest of the crew, which included the talented and versatile young Warwick Rooklyn

Test-fly for a new big spinnaker

as forward hand. As we raced past North Head and out to sea it quickly became obvious that Hot Bubbles' full shape forward did not like meeting waves and we were slipping back in the fleet. Then we messed up the spinnaker set. The cursing Miller's arm-waving gesticulations fired an expensive watch from his wrist into the Tasman Sea. 'You would be the worst (expletive deleted) crew I have ever sailed with,' he

Bob and Craig unpacking a spinnaker for testing / WHITWORTHS ARCHIVE

screamed and stormed down below where he shook with anger for some time while we sailed on.

Miller as always soon forgave us and later he even invited me to join the crew of Apollo III for the 1974 Sydney-Hobart race. Alan Bond vetoed that opportunity; there was no way he would have a journalist on board and in a way, he did me a favour as the boat was to be a flop. Apollo III had a great crew with Miller the skipper and principal helmsman and a nucleus from Ginkgo; Richard Hammond, Pod O'Donnell, Dick Sargeant, Carl Ryves and Alan Norman.

But she was late being launched, despite the best efforts of her building team headed by Trevor Gowland at Halvorsen Gowland's factory in Wyong. The keel was built in aluminium and the lead melted into it on the water's edge at McCarr's Creek, Pittwater, shortly before Apollo III was launched, only eight days before the start of the Sydney-Hobart race.

Although she finished sixth on corrected time, Apollo III suffered some irritating breakdowns, the worst of these the failure of a bracket holding the steering system. The yacht had to be steered with the emergency tiller on a reach while repairs were made. More seriously, she proved to be badly out of balance and therefore difficult to steer in a

Ballyhoo in 1975 / ROSS

race that had a westerly gale in Bass Strait with 30-40 knots gusting over 50, with big seas. 'I got off it straight after Hobart,' said Ryves. 'It wouldn't steer, had too much weather helm and would broach reaching in 15 knots of wind.'

Richard Hammond remembers Apollo III as being so out of balance that it would round up shy reaching under spinnaker in light air. And he recalls' Miller's frustration with the boat on that Hobart race. Down off Freycinet Peninsula Hammond, Bond and Miller were gathered around the radio, listening to the positions sked. Bond said, 'Bobby, what do you think is wrong with this boat; we are not going so well?'

'Because it's a f'cking great dog, Bondy!'

Before the Admiral's Cup trials in March 1975, Miller reduced Apollo III's handicap rating from 43.1ft by removing 1,500 lb of lead from the keel; building out the forward waterline beam measurement and deck measurement with micro balloons. But although she was fast in light winds and very fast reaching and running in moderate to fresh winds, she was unable to equal the pace upwind of the slightly smaller new Frers 53-footer Bumblebee 3, owned by John Kahlbetzer. Peter Kurts' Sparkman & Stephens 47 Love & War won the trials from Patrice III (Ray Kirby) a newer S&S 47. Bumblebee 3 was third on a tie-break of placings from Ted Kaufman's new self-designed 42-footer Mercedes IV.

Apollo III was fifth, a big 12.5 points gap behind Mercedes IV. Raga-muffin was sixth, another three and a-half points behind. After Ragamuffin withdrew from the Hobart race with a broken intermediate stay in her rig, Fischer initiated heavy surgery on the aluminium hull; pinching in at the after-girth measurement, deepening forward depth and broadening the beam but the performance was never there. Although the boat was fast upwind, she was difficult to control downwind in fresh wind and painfully slow running in light wind. Geronimo, late in arrival from Greece, was short of preparation time, could not sail to her rating in light winds and withdrew from two races.

Ballyhoo racing to Hobart / IAN MAINSBRIDGE

Another Olympic 484, Ceil V owned by Bill Turnbull the former owner of Ceil III, made the 1975 Hong Kong Admiral's Cup team. More Opposition, a near sister Miller 48, built in aluminium for Tony Morgan, was reserve for the British team. All seemed short of sail area and Miller told me much later that he had wrongly located the keel on this generation of boats.

The one Miller design built in 1974 that succeeded was Ballyhoo, greatly helped by owner Jack Rooklyn's persistence with a boat that was initially disappointing. Rooklyn, enthused by the success of the 57ft Apollo, which he still owned, wanted a boat big enough to contest line honours in the world's major races but a 'mini-sized' maxi that could be handled by not too large a crew. Miller sketched the concept lines on a table cloth at the Cruising Yacht Club of Australia over lunch with Rooklyn and yacht broker Bob Holmes.

Ballyhoo was 72ft overall with a shape similar in concept to Apollo and Ginkgo; slender with a long waterline and narrow waterline beam.

She had a conventional sloop rig where the bigger American maxis on the international circuit at that time - Windward Passage, Kialoa and Ondine III - were all two-masted. Bob Holmes, the Sydney yacht broker who negotiated the sale of Apollo by Alan Bond to Rooklyn, organised the initial crew on Apollo for Rooklyn and sailed on the boat for a time.

Ballyhoo, initially proclaimed a 'flop' by Jack Rooklyn, went on to a successful international career after being fitted with a new keel, designed by Alan Payne and Doug Peterson and sail-plan modifications by Californian sailmaker Watts. She won the Hong Kong to Manila China Seas handicap and line honours double in 1976.

Later that year she defeated the top US maxi Kialoa (Jim Kilroy) with two straight wins in the California Cup match-racing series in the California Cup, then again beat Kialoa and Windward Passage in the St Francis Perpetual Trophy. She returned to Australia to take line honours in the 1976 Sydney-Hobart race and sailed on to England where she won line honours in the 1977 Fastnet race. Rooklyn sold her to Bill Whitehouse-Vaux who continued to race her internationally under Bermudan registry with a new name, Mistress Quickly. Rooklyn praised Miller as a 'tremendous designer for speed and lines, he never quite took the engineering into consideration and the factors that a boat meets in ocean racing'.

AFTER THE 1974-75 Australian season Miller spent the northern hemisphere summer in England where he helped John Oakley tune the Olympic 484 Ceil V, which Oakley was skippering for Bill Turnbull and their one-off sister Tony Morgan's More Opposition, both programmed for the 1975 Admiral's Cup. While More Opposition showed great

reaching speed and promise in fresh conditions early in the season she was not suited by the lighter winds that prevailed for the British Admiral's Cup team trials. Miller and Oakley worked hard on improving her handicap and her all-round speed. She missed out on selection, was named as reserve for the three-yacht team but subsequently raced in the Admiral's Cup for the Swiss team under charter.

Bob and Yvonne Miller that summer lived in the flat owned by yachting journalist Jack Knights on the upper floor of an apartment building called Thornhill, on the hill behind the Royal Yacht Squadron and with great views of the Solent. Knights, who had moved from Cowes to a hobby farm at nearby Newport on the Isle of Wight and Miller were good friends and kindred spirits; intelligent, slightly eccentric and sharing a love of fast cars. Jack had an ancient Ferrari, which was suffering from neglect, in the barn at the farm. Bob and Yvonne drove it to Scotland and back, with Miller later reck-

Opposite and this page: Ballyhoo / ROSS

oning that it used up as much brake fluid as petrol on the journey.

Bob enjoyed the English sailing scene that summer, says his friend John ('Chink') Longley, a Perth sailor who had been in Alan Bond's crews aboard Apollo II in her 1973 Admiral' Cup campaign and Southern Cross at the America's Cup in 1974. Miller suggested to More Opposition owner Tony Morgan that he add both Longley and Perth boatbuilder Steve Ward to strengthen the crew, which comprised mainly Morgan's friends and business acquaintances. 'He was mad keen for More Opposition to do well and felt that unless it did, he was finished as a yacht designer,' said Longley. 'But he was not morose or strung up. He was fun to sail with and was enjoying the summer.'

The Admiral's Cup in the 1970s was the epicentre of international offshore racing and the proving ground for the world's best yacht designers: Olin Stephens, Dick Carter, German Frers Jr, Frans Maas, Doug Peterson, Bruce Farr, were all there in 1975 to either watch others fight for their professional lives on the water or sail on their own creations. In 1975 it attracted 19 teams with 300 entries in the Fastnet race, the jubilee event in celebration of the first in 1925. But light winds and strong tides made it a difficult event. Great Britain won easily from Germany with the USA fourth. Australia was a lowly ninth with the Swiss team, including More Opposition, tenth.

Miller sailed aboard his own design Guia III, the former Ginkgo now owned by Giorgio Falck, in the Italian team and now much faster in light weather with more sail area on a taller mast. Showing great offwind speed, she was first to finish in the second inshore race for the RSYS Trophy, which ended in a light-air drifter and second on corrected time. Italian crewmen, celebrating the line honours win, jumped overboard to the applause of spectators on the Cowes promenade.

Neither Ceil 5, racing in the Hong Kong team, nor More Opposition in the Swiss team, performed well in this light-air Admiral's Cup. John Longley recalled: 'More Opposition was a nice boat and really quick when it blew over 18 knots but was a dog in the light to moderate; it was simply underpowered. Indeed, nearly all of Ben's boats of the period suffered from the same problem. He got away with it with Ginkgo and Apollo 2 because they were in a way breakthrough boats in hull form but when Ginkgo was bought by the Italians they immediately put another six feet on the mast. Southern Cross and More Opposition were simply underpowered. That most likely was an overhang from Ben's formative years in Australia where it is windy.

'It was really not until Australia (Alan Bond's 1977 America's Cup challenger) when Ben realised that in the northern hemisphere you need lots of sail. We finished third in the British Admiral's Cup trials but they did not pick us because of our weakness in the light and they thought, correctly, that it was going to be a light summer. We ended up sailing for the Swiss. That was where I learned that great Swiss for'ard hand saying: 'You know sailing is like bobsledding. It is the man at the back that uses the brakes.'

Miller in Cowes also renewed his friendship with Sir Max Aitken, first formed in 1969 when Sir Max's Crusade took line honours in the Hobart race with Alan Bond's Miller-designed Apollo second. He worked on Sir Max's boat Perseverance and became a frequent visitor to Sir Max's famous pink house, The Prospect, on the Cowes waterfront. Sir Max was the son of Lord Beaverbrook, the newspaper baron who was a member of Sir Winston Churchill's wartime cabinet. He succeeded his father as chairman of Beaverbrook newspapers, publisher of the Daily Express and Evening Standard. Sir Max was a Squadron Leader during World War Two, decorated with the DSO and DFC, credited with shooting down 14 enemy aircraft. Among Ben's favourite stories about Sir Max was the following, relayed by John Longley:

Ben: 'Hey Sir Max, how did you manage to survive the whole war as a Spitfire pilot when the average life expectancy was three weeks?'

Sir Max: 'Well I went and bought a brand-new Spitfire off my father and then went and hired myself a really good instructor who taught me how to fly it properly; at a time when most kids were getting a total of nine hours instruction if they were lucky. I then flew it to an RAF airfield and joined up, complete with plane.

'The trick was that when you went on a mission most of the time you did not see much but if you saw a German you had to very quickly figure out whether the guy could fly or not. If he could you buggered off asap. If he was hopeless you shot him down.'

Longley adds: 'I have no idea if this is really what Max told him, whether he was pulling Ben's leg or Ben was making it up, but it certainly made the weather rail great fun.'

THE MILLER AND Whitworth partnership foundered on the establishment of an English branch of Miller & Whitworth in association with British sailmaker John Oakeley at Titchfield, near Southampton, in 1974. From there, the confident young Australians planned to service the European market with designs, sails, and Australian-made masts and fittings. Miller intended to fulfil a long-held dream of spending half of the year working and sailing in Europe and the other half in Australia.

Craig Whitworth with the company's general manager Robert Thompson and Sarah Ferguson, the sail assembly supervisor at the Brookvale loft, went to England to establish the branch, just after the 1974 America's Cup. Whitworth returned to Australia in mid-1975 because the business in Sydney was not going so well and the European venture was beginning to look like the impossible dream, while Bob and Yvonne Miller stayed in England.

Looking back 30 years later from the pinnacle of heading a boat fittings retail chain of shops throughout Australia with a staff of 150 people, Whitworth said: 'I wouldn't dream of trying to do something in England. It was madness; it just got out of control.'

Whitworth reflecting on their split, said: 'He was working with Oakeley and then he was back here. There was no discussion between us that he wasn't happy and he was going. But in typical Bob fashion, I just realised he hadn't shown up for a fair while.'

He does not look back on their association with any regrets. 'Not at all, Bob and I had so much fun together, we really did. We had dramas too, but we had a lot of fun. We enjoyed sailing together. I haven't got any regrets about it although I am not saying it wasn't hard.'

A reason for Miller splitting from the partnership may have been a perception that Whitworth was getting more out of it financially. 'We were 50/50 in the sailmaking and the yacht design, which was a spin-off from the sailmaking,' said Whitworth. 'What money was in to start the business, I'd put in. After a couple of years, I realised Bob wasn't going to be the most stable guy to have in business with you and I decided to start another business just retailing boat fittings. At that time, Bob had a minority interest, which he didn't pay for. I had a background in retailing with my dad, I liked doing it and wanted to build it up; it didn't take my efforts away from the rest of the company.

'And somewhere down the track somebody told Bob he was being taken advantage of and should be 50/50 in everything. But they were people who didn't really know Bob and how it all worked. I can say without hesitation that Bob didn't get a bad deal from me, ever. I supported him to the end. He was a great character; the sort of guy who in earlier times would have been the court jester. I have never known anybody who could so easily engage people. If I was to meet Warren Buffet or Bill

Gates, it would be a very formal, stunted sort of a conversation because I would be too aware of their position. But Bob would have them laughing and be invited to join them for the weekend.

'The really wealthy in Europe, like Giorgio Carrera and Giorgio Falck, just loved him because he was so amusing. But they also never saw his dark side. He may not have been bipolar but what they are describing in recent times as bipolar sounds a bit like Bob. One day he'd be saying, 'We're going to win the world' and then the next day he would be in the depths of depression.'

After he realised Miller had gone, Whitworth decided to get out of yacht design, sailmaking and spar making to concentrate on just selling boat equipment. Gary Gietz, who had been working at Miller & Whitworth, took over the sailmaking business to start Olympic Sails. Whitworth sold the sailmaking/design premises, paid off the mortgage, took a shop on the other side of Warringah mall for his retailing activities. 'I love retailing, knew a bit about it and felt no-one else in Australia was doing it right in boating and that's where it started. We now have 16 shops around Australia, 150 staff and a nice management structure. I am still involved as chairman but there is no job for me to do in there. If I fell under a bus, the whole thing would still keep going.'

Whitworth scouts for new shop locations, evaluates produce and provides his experience and guidance when necessary. He has a Palm Beach 50 motor cruiser and plays a lot of golf. 'I really enjoy it as a complete away from the marine industry. We are still looking to expand; get a bit bigger and a bit stronger.'

# 9

# ENTER BEN LEXCEN

ALAN BOND, UNLIKE MILLER, WAS far from downcast over the America's Cup whitewash of 1974. He still saw the America's Cup as an ongoing business opportunity as well as a sporting challenge. Late in 1975 he was on the 'phone to Miller in Cowes, asking him to design another Twelve Metre. Miller refused but Bond kept calling.

Bond finally turned up in Cowes and confronted Miller in the supermarket, where Miller used to say he was spending his last few bob on a packet of cornflakes. He persuaded Miller to design him a new America's Cup challenger. To do that Miller, in December 1975, formed a partnership with Johan Valentijn, a talented young Dutch designer who had been working for Sparkman & Stephens in New York under Olin Stephens for nearly five years.

Their first projects were a One Tonner for Gary Bogard, Ginkgo's original owner and a Half Tonner for limited production design in Italy. Miller had the satisfaction, while returning to Sydney for Christmas, of seeing his One Tonner design Rampage, a sister to Ceil III, win the 1975 Sydney-Hobart race. Owner/skipper Peter Packer from Perth and his son Ron, who navigated, altered the original One Ton configuration by adding mast height and increasing ballast to improve performance in light to moderate weather.

Miller returned to England to begin seven months of methodical work with Valentijn on Bond's new Twelve Metre. They analysed the wind and wave conditions over a number of previous years for the race course area off Newport during the July-September period of the challenger elimination races and the America's Cup. This encouraged them to design a boat for light to moderate winds which, they calculated, prevailed at Newport for more than 70 per cent of the time through the Cup regattas period.

They made an intensive computer analysis of the Twelve Metre rule, studied a number of successful and less successful Twelve Metres and progressively made and tested six models of the largest possible size at scale 1:9 (2.25m overall) that could be tested in the towing tank of Delft University in The Netherlands. The models included ones of the 1974 contestants Southern Cross and Courageous. The testing, combined with analysis of the 1974 races allowing for crewing and tactical mistakes, showed that in 12 knots of breeze Southern Cross was theoretically 25 seconds slower than Courageous on a windward leg and 15 seconds slower on a downwind leg.

The new Twelve, initially labelled Southern Cross II, was smaller and lighter by some 8000 lb (3629kg) and carried 70sq ft (21.33sq m) more sail area than the original Southern Cross. The shape was conventional, more in the style of the Sparkman & Stephens' designed Courageous and Columbia. She was slightly firmer in the midships section and finer in the run aft than Courageous. The shape where the keel met the hull was more tightly radiused and the lead ballast keel was bulbed more markedly, so the centre of gravity was lower.

The designers' tank testing and studies indicated that the new boat would be considerably faster than Southern Cross to windward and on reaches and runs at least equal to Courageous 1974 in the light to moderate winds expected on the Newport course area, but no faster than Southern Cross in winds of 20 knots and more. Months of trialling in Australia later supported the designers' conclusions.

Miller and Valentijn besides designing the boat had to organise a boatyard to build it after negotiations with British yacht builder Joyce

Ben Lexcen (right) and Johan Valentijn study
the plans of Australia / JON SIMONDS

Marine Brothers, of Southampton, fell through.
Later in 1976 they moved
to Perth where Alan
Bond provided them with
an empty warehouse in
Osborne Park and allowed
them to buy all the necessary tools and hire a building team headed by Steve
Ward, then only 23, who
had left the family boat-
building business to go
sailing with Alan Bond on
Apollo II and Apollo III
and who also sailed More
Opposition in the English
summer of 1975. Luck-
ily, he was joined by New
Zealander Brian Riley
who happened to stop by on his way travelling through Australia. He
had worked for seven years building aluminium racers for Steel Yachts
and Launches in Auckland.

They completed the boat in six months, including setting up the
yard and according to Valentijn, the yacht rated as high in quality, if not
higher, than the US-built boats.

Alan Bond and Miller were already close friends, but from the time
Bond engaged him to design his 1977 challenger Miller became virtually
another member of the Bond family. Bond made him financially secure
and whenever Miller was in Perth he stayed at the Bond family home at
Dalkeith with Alan and Eileen Bond and their four children: Susanne,
Jodie, John and Craig.

It was a chaotic place with the Bonds following many separate interests. It had a cellar bar and banquet hall where Alan Bond entertained
his business acquaintances and an underground car park with a big and
varied collection of vehicles from a Rolls Royce to sports cars. 'You just
take whichever one that has petrol in it,' Miller used to say. 'If Eileen
runs out of petrol, she just leaves the car, takes a taxi home and picks up
another one.'

BOND'S SECOND CHALLENGE was leaner and far less obtrusive than the first. Only one boat would go to Newport while he had shipped two Twelves, Gretel II as well as Southern Cross, in 1974 with a team of 45 people at an all-up cost said to be about $4.5 million. The 1977 team was 20; 11 crew members, two reserves and support personnel. With his Bond Corporation financially stretched at the time, Bond also sought public support and major sponsorship through a company he formed called America's Cup Challenge '77 Ltd to co-ordinate public fund raising and sponsorship. Even naming the new boat was an earner, from a public competition carrying a small entry fee. And this time, with rival challengers and the American defence candidates already committed, there was no secrecy surrounding the design and building of the new boat.

About the time the new Bond boat was christened Australia, on February 27, 1977, Miller changed his name by deed poll to Ben Lexcen, prompting his old friend Jack Knights to write: 'The naming competition should have been devoted instead to naming the designer.' Miller changed his name because John Oakley in Britain, after Whitworth's departure, had continued to not only make sails under the Miller & Whitworth name but market designs which were not Miller's. A young graduate from the Southampton Yacht Design Faculty had joined Oakeley as a designer, with their first boat a three-quarter tonner. He was Ed Dubois, later to make his own name as a designer of successful offshore racers and then, superyachts. His Vanguard, designed under the M&W

Australia under construction / JON SIMONDS

label for David Lieu of Hong Kong, was one of the outstanding yachts of the 1977 Admiral's Cup series.

Typically, Miller gave various reasons for selecting Lexcen as his new name, including a search of the Readers' Digest computer bank to find a name that no-one else had. Yvonne Lexcen said the name came from her mother's family. Her long-haired dachshund was called Benji.

And while Jim Hardy was trying and failing to put together his own syndicate to challenge through the Royal Sydney Yacht Squadron, Bond chose Noel Robins, 41, who was the current Australian champion in the Soling class, to skipper Australia. Robins, from Perth, was partly paralysed in the legs from the time he broke his neck in a car accident when he was 21. But that had not stopped him from being a top 14ft skiff sailor and a successful businessman. Classified as a walking quadriplegic, he would later skipper the gold medal winning team at the 2000 Sydney Paralympic Games. Sadly, he died in 2003 after being hit by a car as he crossed a road in Perth.

The crew, mostly from Western Australia, included as alternate helmsman Sydneysider David Forbes, the 1972 Olympic gold medallist in the Star class, who had sailed in Hardy's Gretel II crew in the 1970 challenge and American Andy Rose as tactician. They trained and trialled Australia against Southern Cross off Yanchep for two months from mid-February 1977, with Lexcen usually steering Southern Cross. While Gordon Ingate had mounted a challenge through the Royal Sydney Yacht Squadron with a re-vamped Gretel II, the Australian syndicates from east and west prepared in isolation, later in Newport as well as Australia; ultimately a telling factor against Australia.

Ben makes a point to Scott McAllister and John Longley / JON SIMONDS

Racing off Yanchep, over a short triangular/windward-leeward course with 2n mile windward beats, Australia performed as Miller and Valentijn's research had predicted and even exceeded their expecta-

Benny and the Jets: Benny steering Southern Cross, Jack Baxter foreground / ROSS

tions in stronger winds.

I visited Yanchep to watch some of the trials and recorded these impressions of Australia and the training scenario: 'She has a tiny hull, big rig, is lively in the lightest winds, manoeuvrable, accelerates quickly, stable in a moderate-fresh breeze and has a very low pitching moment. Over the two days racing I watched the new yacht win every start and every race against Southern Cross.

'The whole operation at Yanchep is much more open-handed and relaxed than in 1974 when I hid in the bushes and aboard a cray fishing boat to watch Southern Cross' early sailing and had furtive meetings in the evenings with Bob Miller. Access this time is unlimited and Bob, now Ben, even invites me aboard Southern Cross for the day's sailing against Australia: 'Come with us, we've only got 13 today.'

'THE CREW ON the warm-up boat calls itself 'Benny and the Jets' after the Elton John hit of the time. 'The Jets' are mostly youngsters eager to learn, sights set on the next challenge or gathering experience for big-yacht ocean racing. With as many as five them at times fighting to do the same job, sailing with them is entertaining.

'Benny is calmer than the old Bob Miller. He's had a health scare – high blood pressure – but is getting over that with medication, and a much more relaxed outlook on life (well that's what I think before the racing starts).

'And he is really sailing this boat well. The mainsail leech looks shot with stretch distortion but the general shape is not bad. A recut six-ounce headsail looks good and is proving to be an effective sail through a wide range and he had added inner sheeting tracks which have improved Southern Cross' light air performance.

'Australia is going faster today with more mast bend, thanks to the removal of the jumpers. She catches us port and starboard on the line in one start through her smaller turning circle and slow trim by The Jets but we sail on and gain the lead when Australia's crew fouls a sheet through grinding a loose spinnaker sheet through the genoa block and has to tack away to clear it.

'Australia rolls us over quite easily in the second race, really fast to windward in 10 to 12 knots. Then her crew has problems with the twin-grooved headfoil while trying to change genoas as the wind increases over 15 and loses us.

'Now it's The Jets' turn for drama. We have to change to a heavier headsail, too. A wave picks up the old sail as it is being unbanked and washes it overboard, taking one of The Jets with it. We pick him up and in the process another Jet goes over the side.

'Then Benny is displeased with The Jet manning the spinnaker pole topping lift. 'If you don't get your head up out of that hatch and have a look next time you have to lift that pole, I'll come up there and knock it off your shoulders,' he says, sounding just like the old Bob Miller. We return to the harbour for lunch.

'There are no fancy tenders in this no-frills campaign. The boats sail in and out of the very narrow entrance and dock. A launch with only one of its two engines working is ready to tow them out again.

'We race once more. This time we start ahead and to leeward in about eight knots. Within 400 yards Australia sails straight over the top of us. We throw a few tacks, they cover and keep going away, vastly superior. Benny mutters: 'I'm not really aggressive today; I've taken too many blood pressure pills.' The Jet manning the topping lift might not agree.

'We cannot make any impression on Australia, even though we cheat and bear away 200 yards short of the windward mark. Then Benny tries to put The Jets through a spinnaker gybe/set that ends in a gigantic mess. The problem is not helped by Benny and Ron Packer, the navigator/tactician, yelling conflicting instructions at the foredeck and then yelling at each other in something that sounds like a passage from Grand Opera as each realises the other has different views on how it should be done.

'With Australia long gone, The Jets try again, step by step, and again there's a mess-up with the brace catching in a jib hank and two now thoroughly stirred up Jets fighting on the point for the privilege of releasing it.

'Benny soon cools it down, starts a long and funny monologue about his experiences with the telephone system in Italy and with the breeze dropping right out, both boats return to the marina.'

Alan Bond told me during that visit: 'To suggest we are in a financially embarrassed position is quite wrong. Everything we have done is paid for and nothing has been spared in spending on the boat. There's never been any thought that we cannot afford this sail or that sail. Nothing has been wasted either. We have not been able to support the crews to the extent we have done before but it has not affected the line-up of guys who want to be on the boat.

'There's no fuss about this effort, you know. This has been just a quiet, let's go sailing type of series.'

On Australia's chances in the America's Cup, Bond said: 'I think we have an even-money chance of winning it. We were about five-to-one last time.'

But preparing in isolation at home and later in Newport, where the Swedish Sverige challenging syndicate reneged on an earlier promise to tune and train against the Australians, were to greatly lessen those odds. Australia may have been an outstanding design but sail-shaping and rig tuning were to let her down. Her crew was a good one but lacked the ultimate sharpness achieved by the Americans through a hard-fought defender trials series. Scott McAllister was on the bow, John Longley

Australia and Southern Cross training off Yanchep / ROSS

Benny / ROSS

sailed sewer, Mike Summerton ran the mast, John Phillips and John Rosser were the grinder hands. Lee Killingworth was port trimmer and Norm Hyett starboard trimmer. David Forbes trimmed the main, Andy Rose was the tactician, Jack Baxter was the navigator and Noel Robins drove. Ross Annear and Wayne McCurry were back-up crew. Steve Ward looked after the boat with Richard Goldsmith as a 'gopher'. John Fitzhardinge, who was the Commodore of the Sun City Yacht Club, through which Australia challenged, was also the rigger. Sailmaker Rob Antill was joined in Newport by Ian Broad from Hood sails. Warren Johns was manager.

In the challenger eliminations at Newport, Australia beat Baron Bich's ageing France 4-0 while Gretel II went down 3-4 to Sverige, designed and skippered by Pelle Petterson. Then Australia beat Sverige 4-0 in the final.

But in the Cup, Australia was no match for a re-vamped Courageous which, skippered by Ted Turner, again won the US defender trials over new boats Enterprise (Lowell North) and Independence (Ted Hood). Courageous beat Australia 4-0 by margins of 1min 48sec, 1:03 2:32 and 2:25.

Lexcen, although earlier named as a reserve, had to pay his own way to Newport. In an interview there with his yachting journalist friend Lou d'Alpuget, he aired his frustrations: 'We went into it this year with the wrong frame of mind – starry eyed and over-confident – after we'd beaten the French and the Swedes.

'I arrived in Newport a week before the series against Courageous and after one sail on Australia I told our crew our headsails were too flat high up and too full down low and that our mast was not in tune. It

The Twelves' base at Yanchep, 1977 / ROSS

was sagging 15 inches to leeward at the top and robbing the mainsail of power, thus making the boat stand up straight and look tremendously stiff, which in fact she is not.

'Only Bondy himself would take me seriously but the rest of the team – and I've got to include our skipper Noel Robins and our very experienced sheet hand David Forbes beside him in the cockpit – didn't want to hear my views. I was told it would be much better if I didn't come out in the boat with them again because I was a disturbing influence. So, I took Bondy out in his tender to watch Courageous in her final training and showed him the difference between her sails and ours. But even he could not persuade the afterguard on Australia that changes were needed.

'Although our sailmaker Robbie Antill (of North Sails Australia) worked his heart out, we finished up with only one headsail (a 4oz) anywhere near the correct special shape for a Twelve Metre. Looking from astern our headsails up high were nearly as flat as knife blades. At the best, they had a draft of 10 per cent and looked very much like IOR boats' sails. 'Courageous' headsails were much fuller up high with a minimum of 13 per

Australia off Yanchep / ROSS

Australia training with Southern
Cross, Yanchep / ROSS

cent draft and they were sheeted in with the leech only six inches away from the spreaders. Ours hung 2ft away from the spreaders. I told our people either we or the Americans must be wrong and that at least we should try, even as an experiment, with some headsails like theirs. They wouldn't listen.

'Robbie Doyle (of Hood Sails USA), Courageous' sail trimmer, who made her sails, and Ted Hood himself, told me later that they had known as soon as they had seen Australia's headsails that she'd never be able to point with the defender. They'd been worried earlier because they believed our hull form was at least the equal of Courageous, possibly faster as our tank tests had told us. Ted Turner could squeeze up from leeward of us whenever we got within range in the same weight and direction of wind. We made other mistakes too, minor ones of tactics, helmsmanship and handling, whereas the Americans were just about perfect after months of hard match racing and tuning.

Australia leads Southern Cross / ROSS

'Perhaps on that account alone they'd have beaten us, even if we had facsimiles of Courageous' sails. But we robbed ourselves of a show because of our sails and because we stuck with the mast out of Southern Cross and left a new spar that had never been properly tested with $30,000 worth of superb rigging on it, on the dock.'

Johan Valentijn soon

after the 1977 America's Cup left the partnership with Lexcen to work for Baron Bich in Paris on a new Bich challenger for the 1980 America's Cup. In a retrospective article he distributed to sailing publications, he explained that time had simply run out on the new mast. The Southern Cross mast, developed by John Bertrand after testing a whole series of shapes in the Sydney University civil engineering department, was basically triangular in section shape and of riveted aluminium construction.

The Southern Cross campaign had spent a lot of money on researching that shape. 'The section they ended up with might have been good or bad,' said Valentijn. 'Enthusiastically we thought we ought to study those tests once more to see if we could not pick up something new (we were not 100 per cent convinced of the all-round performance (of the Southern Cross section). But what a disappointment to find out there were no records of this whole expensive effort.

'As time was running short we decided that we must be able to do better with just some common sense. We figured that we could design a simple, close to elliptical, mast with 150lb of lead in the bottom to make it both minimum in weight and CG height. This meant a CG 2.5ft lower than the so-called super-section mast used on Southern Cross.'

Getting the mast built in Australia, like building the boat, meant starting from scratch. 'After convincing everybody that the 'impossible' was possible, work on the die was started. Due to a number of factors beyond our control we finally got the sections some four months later than originally promised. As time was running out this job had to be rushed. It finally got finished in Newport. Due to time and other problems it was decided to keep the old Southern Cross mast in the boat. Who says a 1000 lb mast with a 2.5ft lower C of G and less frontal area is an advantage anyway! I guess I wasn't persuasive enough and there remained a tuning problem.'

Valentijn said one of the problems with the North sails was a directive from the New York Yacht Club forbidding exchange of information between US and foreign lofts. 'We were left without all the experience gained on Intrepid, never mind the new Enterprise,' he said. 'To make matters worse, it was decided by the syndicate to keep practising with the only three new sails it had bought while old Southern Cross sails filled up the gap.

'When we finally got sailing off Rhode Island (after a 14-week layoff), we quickly learned that Twelve Metre sails don't set 'straight out of the bag'. Some of them did look pretty good but all needed work. Rob Antill from

Australia training Yanchep / ROSS

North, Sydney, together with mainsheet hand Dave Forbes, got down to a very systematic approach. They photographed every single sail to get the shape and compared this with what they felt were relatively fast sails, or what they felt from intuition or past experience would be better.

'As we did not have any good competition, we were left to improve boat speed from past performance recorded on tapes. By constantly working on the sails we improved the boat speed all around by as much as 0.4 knots in six knots of true breeze and 0.15 in 15 knots of breeze. If we could have been pressed for competition by boats like Enterprise or Independence and had a few more months, I'm convinced the sailmakers would have been able to improve more. Two months is not very much time to come up with the ideal sails for the world's best competition.

'We were running so late that three days before the America's Cup series three new jibs and one new main arrived from Sydney. We did some minor work on all of them. They had the shape we had learned was best, yet the America's Cup course and series is neither the place nor the time for experiment. We thought they were better than the old sails but we didn't know for sure.'

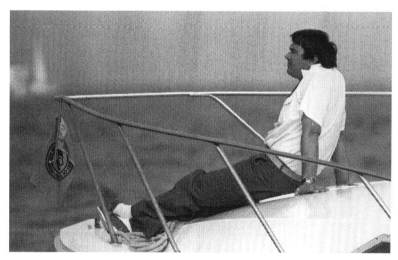

Ben watches the last race in Newport

# 10

# THE BENDY MAST

A LAN BOND IN OCTOBER 1978 committed to challenging for the America's Cup in 1980, again with Australia but with a much stronger preparation forged around a growing body of experienced crew members and administrators from his two previous campaigns. The challenge this time was made through the Royal Perth Yacht Club and based at the Fremantle Sailing Club's new marina where it enjoyed much more readily available infrastructure support than at the Yanchep housing resort, which Bond had sold to Japanese interests. Australia spent six months' sailing before being shipped to the USA, compared to five weeks before the 1977 challenge and had raced against Gretel II, by then owned by Gordon Ingate and modified by her designer Alan Payne, in three series of races off Sydney and one off Fremantle.

As in 1977 a company, America's Cup 1980 Ltd, was formed to raise funds for the challenge and to dispel the popular notion that Alan Bond owned Australia and its challenge. Warren Jones, executive director of the challenge, said: 'The company was formed so that we could go to the people of Australia and campaign Australia as a people's boat.'

Ben, who with Yvonne had returned to Sydney and resumed living in their house atop the hill at Seaforth overlooking Middle Harbour, went to Perth in October 1978 to sail aboard Australia and plan alterations to her underbody, which made her better balanced and so able to carry more powerful sails, sheeted on harder, to make her a much faster boat upwind. Comments from the Bond camp on those alterations were guarded at the time. But three decades later key crewman John ('Chink') Longley recollected: 'The boat was a woofer upwind (in 1977) but was quicker than Courageous downwind so we only lost by an average of one and a-half minutes rather than over four with the Sudden Curse (Southern Cross). Benny fixed the boat up for 1980 by cutting the whole bustle out and redesigning one that worked. From then on the boat was a honey and if we had been good enough we could have won with her in 1980.'

While working on the design alterations to Australia in 1978, Lexcen became busy with another design project. One day in 1978 he dropped down from his home to visit sailing journalist Rob Mundle, who was also then operating a yacht brokerage, Rob Mundle Sailboat Centre at the Spit. 'He said he was bored with the America's Cup design work and was looking for something totally different to do,' said Mundle, who had been impressed by magazine reports of American Gary Hoyt's Freedom 40 cat-rigged ketch, said, 'Why not do an Australian version of this?'

Lexcen, who on one of his American visits had seen a Freedom 40 slice past a brand new Two Tonner offshore racer on a reach. 'About four weeks later, he pulled up in his old Mercedes and rolled the plans out,' said Mundle.

Lexcen supervised building the first few boats in a fibreglass production run of the Revolution 38 cat ketch,

November 1979 Revolution cat ketch / ROSS

November 1979 Revolution cat ketch / ROSS

which had the foremast set right in the bow and just two sails set on unstayed aluminium masts with wishbone booms, in a Mona Vale factory. Three of the 13 Revolution 38s eventually built were for Ken Berkeley, his friend and crewmate from the 1972 Olympics. Berkeley, who with his brother was running a very successful contract cleaning business in Sydney, had bought the Whitsunday Yachting World charter company. Two of the boats went to a new charter boat business he established in Vanuatu.

The first-launched Revolution 38 attracted much favourable attention at the Sydney Boat Show in August 1979. Three days after that show I am in Fremantle where Lexcen, having his first sail on Australia since the hull alterations, beckons me aboard. If the alterations have corrected the balance problems Australia will not only be easier to steer and track better but also be able to carry more power in her sails and point higher with closer-sheeted headsails. So this outwardly casual-looking sail, with a number of passengers and fill-ins dotted among the crew regulars and the 1977 sails looking tired and stained, is for Lexcen a rather crucial event.

There are only four or five knots of winter wind, the sea is calm and the tension mounts as Lexcen realises that the best mainsail is not aboard and the apparent windspeed component of the Signet digital recording unit, which gives a printed set of data every 12 seconds, is not functioning. But Lexcen's 'I'm going straight home on the next plane' utterance tails off into murmurs of appreciation as the sleek Twelve Metre begins to feed on its apparent wind and gathers speed. 6.79 reads the digital speedo. 'Just trim the main on a little more not but don't flatten it,' says Lexcen quietly to Joe ('The Giant') Cooper, ex Gretel II, now a resident boat Nigel on Australia.

And the little red numbers jump to 6.89, 6.90.

'This was the best jib in 1977,' says Lexcen. 'All the others had the clew up into the block and could not be properly trimmed.'

7.45, 7.50 reads the speedo; we're sailing 32 degrees apparent wind angle.

Ben says the boat feels beautiful and he doesn't need the instrumentation or the best mainsail to tell him the alterations have improved her. 'I thought there were opportunities to improve the shape, to make it more streamlined, just off the seat of my pants. And the place where I made the alterations have also made the boat more like Courageous (the successful Sparkman & Stephens defender of 1974 and 1977). So now, our boat is a small Courageous – very similar in shape – the big difference is that it has less freeboard and is shorter and lighter.'

[The exceptionally low freeboard of the original design lowered the centre of gravity of the hull to increase stability, reduce pitching in rough water and lessened the wind resistance of the hull.]

'I've made the keel sharper in the leading edge, taken some profile off the front of the keel and added it to the back of the trim tab so we don't lose any lateral plane. I altered the bustle [the skeg in front of the rudder] to get the balance right so we can get the rig working properly. I made the bustle deeper and finer, sharper and more streamlined, to give more directional stability and get a bit more lateral plane. The net increase in wetted surface was about two feet, which is not very much. The volume stayed the same and the centre of volume moved aft slightly. Theoretically, moving the centre of buoyancy aft slightly should make the boat better going into a sea and make it balance better. It also gives us a bit more sail area under the rule. I didn't try to affect the rating measurements at all with the changes; it just happened. The measurements just came out that way. The rudder is also deeper and finer.'

Lexcen and Australia's 1977 skipper Noel Robins had intended to sail the boat with the sails and rig in exactly the same trim used in Newport to assess the

Racing Gretel II off Fremantle, 1979 / ROSS

Above: Benny lying down on the job, 1979
Below: Australia March 1980 / ROSS

results of the hull changes by comparing before-and-after instrument printouts. Then they were to assess the elliptical mast made for 1977 but never used. Even without the data comparison, unavailable because of the fault in the wind-speed instrument, Lexcen is convinced that the boat is improved. 'It feels better, tracks better, balances miles better and uses less trim tab. So we will go straight on to test the new mast.'

Lexcen says he will have more say in this challenge than Bond's previous two. 'I am going to be the boat tuner and I am trying to influence the selection of the people. Above all I want to sail on the boat this time. In the previous two challenges I felt my expertise was not in sailing on the boat so someone else might as well do that. But I want to get closer to the problems and know exactly what is going on. Last time when I got over there I was told not to go on the boat as I got too excited and was a disturbing influence. So I got off and never got on again. But I am going to fight tooth and nail to have a say this time.'

Next day Robins sails Australia while Lexcen observes from the tender and says that the hull's flow separation characteristics have improved; the crest of the stern wave is further aft and it is a really full-bodied wave with less turbulence. Robins says the boat is much better balanced. 'We do seem to have got rid of the weather helm.' Warren Jones, the executive director of the challenge syndicate who has been sailing with Robins' crew says on stepping ashore: 'She is going, she is beautiful. I really believe the greatest advantage anyone can have in an America's Cup challenge is experience. I believe we can start from where we finished off last time and just get better.'

After racing against Gretel II off Fremantle in November, Australia was to go to Sydney where, says Lexcen: 'I am going to spend every day on the boat for three months tuning, training, working on the boat so that when it leaves for America there is just nothing left for the crew to do except go sailing.'

However, the racing against Gretel II became less meaningful as Gordon Ingate, who now owned the boat, found difficulty holding experienced crew and it became obvious that Gretel II was no longer fully competitive. Ingate bought her in 1978 and raced her in the Royal Sydney Yacht Squadron's number one division events on Sydney Harbour. He offered to make her available to anyone who wished to try out as helmsman or crew for the 1980 America's Cup. A sub-committee of the syndicate that had backed Ingate's challenge with Gretel II in 1977 tried but failed to form a syndicate to challenge with a new Alan Payne design for 1980.

Ingate shipped Gretel II to England for the Twelve Metre class' first world championship, in September 1979; an event seriously devalued by a warning from the New York Yacht Club that no US Twelve Metre crew, which offered comfort to the enemy by attending the championship need think about competing in the 1980 defence trials. There were only six competitors in the championship, decided on a match-racing format. Britain's new America's Cup challenger Lionheart, an Ian Howlett design skippered by John Oakeley, won by two points from Sweden's Sverige. Gretel II, steered by Graham Newland, was third but with a re-design by Alan Payne to optimise her for light air, was no longer an all-rounder.

In the David Brand Memorial Trophy series, which followed off Fremantle in November 1979 in light-moderate winds Australia, steered by Noel Robins, beat Gretel II with Ingate on the helm in all four races, by

Benny steering / ROSS

margins of 6min 55sec, 5min 42sec, 4min 42sec and 2min 20sec. After that series both boats were shipped to Sydney for more tuning and racing through January, February and March. After the first series of races in January, with Robins, Lexcen and former 18ft skiff champion Bob Holmes alternating on the helm of Australia, the Bond syndicate selected Jim Hardy as its helmsman for the remainder of the campaign. Hardy, who had steered Gretel II for Sir Frank Packer in the eventful 1970 race, in which Gretel II won a race and was disqualified from another after finishing first, had also steered Southern Cross in Bond's spectacularly unsuccessful 1974 campaign.

Through the Sydney series Gordon Ingate had trouble retaining regular crew, with a trip to Newport no longer on the horizon and so

Australia November 1979 / ROSS

Gretel II suffered from handling lapses and breakdowns. With extra ballast added she was at her fastest in the March series, winning two of the six races. But Lexcen said Australia had been deliberately slowed by allowing growth to gather on the bottom. The racing was useful in forging a strong crew for Australia, named after the March series: Team captain Alan Bond (WA) 41, helmsman Jim Hardy (NSW) 47, tactician, Ben Lexcen (NSW) 43, navigator

Jack Baxter (WA) 40, Jock Barker (WA) 35, Rob Brown (NSW) 25, Joe Cooper (NSW) 24, Peter Costello (NSW) 33, Michael Lissiman (WA) 33, John Longley (WA) 34, Scott McAllister (WA) 27, John Rosser (WA) 42, Peter Shipway (NSW) 30, Phil Smidmore (NSW) 26, John Stanley (NSW)

Ben Lexcen steers, skipper Noel Robins in the shade / ROSS

40. Warren Jones, the executive director of America's Cup Challenge 1980 Ltd, managed the team.

THE CREW WAS experienced with even most of the younger members blooded in international competition in ocean racing and various one-design classes. Baxter and Longley had sailed in both the 1974 and 1977 challenges. Lexcen was in general pleased with the progress of the campaign, which he believed would move into a higher gear once the crew reached Newport, away from the distractions and cares of home. 'Basically, the boat is really fast. It is just a matter of knowing what sail to put up at the right time and trying to simplify the wardrobe to two or three headsails and two or three spinnakers.'

As tactician, he was still developing an understanding with Baxter and skipper Hardy. 'Jack Baxter is the perfect navigator because he is not an egotist but just does his job and does it very well,' said Ben. 'And he is a calming influence. I am about the only excitable person on the boat. We have a bunch of guys who are not only hyped up and truly competitive; they are cool. And Jack can cool me down when I get excited. Jim and I are not good together yet because we have not been together long enough but we are getting that way. I am still not skilled enough as a tactician sailing these boats but I will improve.'

The Australia crew left Australia in time for eight weeks' training in Newport, Rhode Island before the elimination series against challengers from England, France and Sweden in August.

Meantime Lexcen in an address on yacht design in a Sailfast seminar in Sydney showed his ability to captivate any audience with insights, away from the text books and accepted theory, on yacht design. He gave it at Woollahra Sailing Club, a progressive dinghy sailing club at Rose Bay on Sydney Harbour. No-one left early.

Here are some excerpts:

*MY FIRST VIEW of the ocean racing scene was, as a boy, watching the start of a Hobart race. There were yachts like Christina, a big, heavy double-ender that won the second Hobart race in 1946. It broke a crosstree before the start and my dentist, Bob Bull, who owned Christina climbed the mast with the spare tiller, which was an axe handle and fitted it as a crosstree. It is probably still there today. Boats of that period had cotton sails and no radios. If it blew hard, instead of belting on as they do these days, the crew would heave to and all go down below and bail out the boat because they used to leak like sieves.*

*Later, while I was designing dinghies, I became interested in bigger boats when the Halvorsen brothers (Trygve and Magnus) began putting together their record of five Hobart race wins (three of them in consecutive years). Their boats actually had carpet on the floor in the main saloon; not a drop of water got inside. They used to win because their boats were strong and they would plug along, perhaps in tenth place, down to Bass Strait where a big southerly would come in and Tryg Halvorsen would stay awake all night and day and belt the hell out of the boat while the other boats were falling apart or the people falling apart. And they would be having hot meals all the way to the Derwent River while the other crews would be lying about in the bilge water of their leaky boats.*

*One of the first successful yachts I designed was Apollo (for Alan Bond). Tryg Halvorsen came with me the first Hobart race we sailed in that boat. We were belting into a pretty big breeze down off Tasmania. I had never designed a boat that big before and I was worried the keel was going to fall off. While they were looking up at the sails, I was down looking under the floorboards. Tryg steered the boat for about 14 hours with an hour's break every now and then from me and half a dozen seasick guys down below. He wasn't that young then and it was really cold. But the old Viking blood was up.*

*Trevor Gowland once told me that in Anitra (Halvorsen brothers' Sydney-Hobart winner of 1957) they sprang a leak in a big sea and water was pouring in. Tryg was steering the boat, pounding along to windward where anyone else would have eased up or turned and run so the boat wouldn't leak so much.*

*Trevor said, 'Tryg, the boat's sinking, the boat's sinking.'*

*Tryg: 'You've got tools?'*

*'Yeah.'*

*'Fix it.'*

*So they kept bashing on.*

*Then through the 1960s Sparkman and Stephens, under the guidance of Olin Stephens, dominated the offshore scene with boats that were wholesome, well designed and properly engineered. The yachts were comfortable for racing and cruising, like Love and War, with good bunks, galley, toilet, shower, where some of the latest boats designed to the International Offshore Rule have really nowhere to sleep, no galley and down below you are up to your armpits in wet sailcloth. It's not very pleasant.*

*Offshore racing has got to the stage where even though the boats are expensive, they are whipped together, filled up with hydraulic gadgets and the crew has to have feet smaller than size nine as there is no room for anyone with size 10 to walk around the deck through the clutter of winches and fittings.*

*I was a bit adventurous at the start of my designing in ocean racing with Ginkgo and Apollo II (1973 Admiral's Cup team yachts) which had no overhangs and a mechanical flush deck layout where boats of that time just had a cockpit down the back and a cabin top.*

*The boats that are sailing now are real machines. I started that machine thing but I am really sad about it when I compare the yachts of today to boats like the original Ragamuffin and beautiful yachts where you could sleep when you were off watch and wake up full of beans to go again.*

*Even American Eagle, the old Twelve Metre, which I sailed down to Hobart with Ted Turner (in 1971 and 1972) had not only real bunks but sheets on the bunks. All the headsails were kept up on deck – you couldn't open the forehatch on a Twelve Metre in the ocean, particularly that one, which was about 5in below its designed waterline and had a 2ft freeboard.*

*All the headsails were lashed on the weather rail. Before a tack, you let the lashings go, the sails all rolled over to leeward and you lashed them on again. Consequently, you never had to open the forehatch which meant the boat never sank. Peter Bowker, the famous navigator/cook, actually slept under the forehatch and had a bed there.*

*It was amusing sailing with the Americans because when I get in a Hobart race, I put my foul weather gear on at the start and leave it on, barring bodily functions, all the way to Hobart. I don't wash, I smell. The smell cannot get out of a good set of foul weather gear; everybody else smells too. This is the Australian way.*

*I was a watch captain, alternating in a bunk with the captain on the other watch, a big guy from Texas, Legree Van Ness. He used to take off his foul weather gear and all his clothes and put on pyjamas to get into the bunk. It would take him half an hour to get ready for the sack and then half to three quarters of an hour to get his gear back on.*

*I used to go off watch, crash straight into the same bunk wringing wet, sleep, get up, go straight on deck. After a couple of days he says: 'There's a leak in the deck here somewhere, the bunk's always wet.' So, you had fun in those old boats that had beds and things. You can't have fun in a boat that's full of water. How could a guy say, 'there's a leak in the deck' when you are up to your eyeballs in wet sails?*

*The IOR is not really handicapping boats, as it was intended to do, but influencing the shape of boats and most of the IOR boats are really dreadful to sail. A successful US-designed IOR boat I sailed on recently would pull your arms out on a wind. Instead of making the hull a nice shape so it won't get out of control downwind, they put a 5ft deep rudder on a nasty hull shape to make it easy to steer. The hull shape is nasty because it suits the rule so the boat can have heaps of sail area and go fast on the wind in light weather. And even then, it is nearly breaking your arm steering as one degree of turn on this 5ft deep by 3ft wide rudder really exerts some foot pounds on the steering wheel.*

*Downwind this 46ft boat never does more than 10 knots except on an extreme wave. We used to do 15 and 16 knots ten years ago and have a great old time! The Bruce Farr boats punched along at 15 to 16 knots but the rules don't like the Farr boats any more.*

*Through history, yacht design has been influenced by rules that some do-gooders have introduced to try and make yachts easier to handicap. It would be a lot cheaper to build a whole lot of nice one designs if you really want to race out in the ocean. You would have close racing instead of belting out of the harbour and having big fun and games with other boats then sailing all the way to Hobart with 140 boats and not seeing another boat from dark on the first night until hitting the Derwent River. That's not fun; that's a race against your brain. To get the blood up, you have to see the competitors, you have to be able* to breathe on them, punch them.

There will always be development ocean racers and there won't be any fewer of these owners – the sport needs them to progress. But there will be many more new people coming into the sport to sail boats like J24s, just as the Hobie cats attracted people to sailing who otherwise would have been playing tennis or riding horses.

I stopped designing ocean racers accidentally because I got involved with the Twelve Metres and now I am married to the damned Twelve Metres, which is a love-hate relationship. The Twelve Metre is a good thing for me, other than it keeps me in bickies in that it is a total design effort. You design the boat, the construction, you build the boat, you make all the fittings because there are no fittings to the standard that you require.

There are no blocks on any yacht in the world as good as the blocks we have on our Twelve Metre. They cost a couple of thousand bucks each.

There is no rigging like we've got. The rod rigging itself represents a saga in logistics. The New York Yacht Club would not allow us to buy the ready-made Navtec rod rigging from the US. So, we had to buy the nickel cobalt by telegram, pay for it from a Swiss bank, ship it across to England, the only place we could find with a machine that could roll it and slowly reduce this great big billet of rare material down to long, thin ribbons, have it sent somewhere else to get the threads rolled on and fly it out to Perth.

The only thing I ignored last time was designing the sails; this time I am getting into that too. The whole project is so complete. You have to teach the crew to sail the boat, paint the boat. In Perth I met a medical professor at the university who is interested in hip joints. During his research he has developed a super slippery surface to make this ball joint work without lubrication. Under an electron scanner this surface looks like plate glass where a paint surface on a Rolls Royce that to the eye looks unbelievably smooth appears under the scanner like the surface of the moon. I have been testing models with this super finish to try and reduce friction on the boat.

All these sorts of fine, abstract things I am involved in now are far and away from the old IOR where you bash out the old similar designs as you are afraid to go too far away from Ron Holland or Doug Peterson as you are going to be out of the ball game – either you make a breakthrough or come a gutser.

You've got to keep plugging away at the America's Cup. It's like buying *a lottery ticket. You don't realise the effort that goes into even losing. Our effort is mammoth and I know it is mammoth for the other challengers.*

*The New York Yacht Club is scared. They would not let a US boat go to the so-called Twelve Metre championship in England as they were frightened it might teach someone how to sail the boats. We have had sailmaking people out from America who could not get onto our boat and look at the sails because they were frightened there would be a photograph in a magazine that the New York Yacht Club would see. It's really war; you cannot believe what it's like. It is a super war with our puny little farm country fighting against the big, bad Americans with their big technology.*

*You really feel the technology gap in Perth, where we built and modified Australia. The only engineering you can buy off the shelf there is for mining or house-building. The smallest bolts you can buy are the inch and a-half Whitworths that go into the front of a D9 cat. You cannot buy any sophisticated stuff like airplane bolts.*

*But we did everything properly and our boat is indestructible. It is very light and frail-looking but it is really strong and nothing on it corrodes.*

*There is no way we can cheat on the restrictions applied to the use of US sail technology, so we are still behind the eight ball. The America's Cup is not easy to win but one day someone will win it. The opposition is getting stronger and now it is getting competitive beforehand. It may not be enough to win this time but one time they will have a weak defence and we will beat them.*

*Adventure is still in my soul, you will be sorry to hear and at the risk of going broke my next project will be the yacht for the year 2050. Development for the yacht of the future will go along two courses. One will be a high-speed catamaran type and the other a sophisticated monohull that suits the times and looks more like an airplane than a boat.*

*Maybe it's something in the rig. The usual method of joining jib and mainsail at the top of the mast isn't the best aerodynamic system; it's only done for mechanical expediency. So maybe having the leading edges of the jib and parallel is the proper thing. Bi-planes didn't have the wings coming together at the wing tips – one did; it crashed.*

*So maybe with more refined materials – maybe with Kevlar, carbon fibre, something not yet discovered, we can make nice unstayed masts with no rigging and make them into semi-wing sails that revolve so you can have a yacht that doesn't need a fence because it doesn't need people walking around the deck.*

It can be round and streamlined like a space-ship and you can sit in a little computerised gadget with a steering wheel and all the controls at your fingertips. That's how I think the yacht of the future will be. It won't be a garbage tip of winches and junk all over the deck with 20 people in super space suits and big brains running around and shouting at each other, pulling ropes.

Australia in Newport / ROSS

I have been racing for 30-odd years and have two big rules I keep belting into my head: If your boat is not going fast, one, ease the sails off and two, flatten the sails out. More boats go slow because their sails are too full than those with sails that are too flat. When I am in trouble in a race I flatten the sails off a bit and ease the sheets off. I am only wrong one time in a 100.

That's it, folks.

Throw fruit!

IN THE EARLY stages of Australia's training and trialling in Newport, Ben exploded famously when he read Australian newspaper reports that John Bertrand was to replace him as tactician. Unbeknown to the rest of the Australian team Bond, with the 1983 campaign already forming in his sub-conscious, invited Bertrand to become tactician. Bertrand, who had won selection in the Australian Olympic team as skipper in the Soling keelboat class, was dealing with the bitter disappointment of the Australian Yachting Federation's decision, at Prime Minister Malcolm Fraser's request, not to send a team to the 1980 Moscow Olympics in protest against Russia's invasion of Afghanistan.

I was editing Australian Sailing magazine at that time. Bertrand, then proprietor of North Sails Melbourne, had been writing a regular

Benny laughs off the broken wrist

column on boat speed for the magazine. Excitedly, he telephoned one day and told me that Bond had offered him the tactician spot and I reported that in a story published in the Sydney Morning Herald.

When the news got to Newport Benny, furious, hit a wall in the Australian team's Newport headquarters so hard that he broke his wrist. He told Jim Hardy: 'Well, after I read the newspaper article I went back into the office and saw Bertrand's face on the wall so I thumped it as hard as I could. I'd seen blokes do that in the movies and I thought I'd try it myself. I guess I'm no movie star. They never broke their wrist.'

Hardy added in his autobiography An Adventurous Life that John Bertrand's superior educational qualifications really frustrated Lexcen. 'Jim, every time I am with John Bertrand, he makes me feel as though I am in an examination. He doesn't seem to realise that I have had only two years at school.'

While Ben had spent only two years at primary school and two at high school, Bertrand had degrees from Monash University in Melbourne and the Massachusetts Institute of Technology in Boston. 'John was very factual whereas Benny was really abstract,' wrote Hardy. 'There was definite friction between them that summer.'

After team manager Warren Jones and Hardy convinced him that replacing Lexcen would seriously disrupt the crew at that late stage, Bertrand reluctantly accepted a sail-trimming role.

Benny, typically, turned the broken wrist setback into a laugh. With marker pen he boldly inscribed a lightning bolt on the cast and the message, 'Today the world, tomorrow the universe.'

Australia in Newport was up against the best-prepared American defence to that time. Dennis Conner had taken the technique of two-boat tuning to its ultimate and into the America's Cup with two very even boats, Freedom and Enterprise, both designed by Sparkman & Stephens, racing against each other for 15 months for a total time on the water of 2100 hours. Eighty sails were made, tested and interchanged between the two boats before Freedom, built initially as a trial horse for Enterprise, was selected as the defender.

The Australians in Newport preparing to meet the awesome Freedom machine first had to beat three other challengers. None of them was offering the sort of competition Enterprise was giving Freedom. Australia was a faster boat than Sweden's Sverige, Britain's Lionheart was badly managed and under-capitalised. France 3 had a fast hull but poor sails because her owner Baron Bich's pride denied her even token acceptance of American sail cloth or sail-making expertise.

Australia / ROSS

Lionheart, however, introduced the 'secret weapon' that Australia adopted, which with more time conceivably could have won the America's Cup. Her innovative designer Ian Howlett and sailmaker skipper John Oakley, in Lionheart's training alliance with Australia before the challenger eliminations, one day come out with a bendy-topped mast and walloped Australia in very light winds. The plastic top on the aluminium mast when severely bent added extra, un-measured sail area.

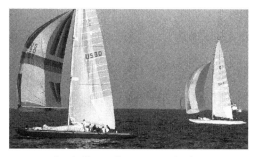

Australia on the way to winning resail race two / ROSS

Benny the tactician / ROSS

Lexcen, always receptive to new ideas, saw it as a way of 'tuning an FJ Holden into a Ferrari'. Skipper Hardy and syndicate head Bond readily agreed to the gamble of adding a longitudinal-strand fibreglass top, about four metres long, to replace the top of one of Australia's aluminium masts. Besides providing 400sq ft of extra sail area, the mainsail peaked in an ellipse, which airplane designers, catamaran, Moth and NS14 dinghy sailors already recognised as being more efficient than the pointed top, which was really an engineering expediency. Ben designed the new mast and had flown in from Sydney the technician who had built the unstayed masts for the Revolution 36 to make the 'glass top. They built the mast in a fishermen's shed on the waterfront, with a small team of three or four men who kept the operation secret, even from the rest of the Australian squad.

Meantime, Australia was struggling to beat Sverige 3-2 in her first series of the challenger eliminations through a combination of breakdowns, including a broken mast and days lost through unfavourable weather. That left her only two spare days before Australia had to meet France, which had beaten Lionheart in the challenger elimination final, with no time to step the bendy mast before that series as originally intended. Australia, obviously quicker than France, beat her 4-1.

Lack of time developing sails for the new rig and building confidence in it through sailing with it was costly for Australia, which went down 1-4 to Freedom. The bent rig gave Australia a superiority in speed over Freedom in winds of less than ten knots that enabled her to win a race, have a chance of winning another and gave her a 700-metre lead in a third race with one leg to go when the time limit ran out. Given more

1980 the bendy mast / ROSS

experience with the rig, Australia could have extended its potency into the medium-strong wind ranges.

Freedom's overall superiority was due not to hull design but to rig and sail design. Freedom's oft-tested, refined sail shapes with large mainsail roaches supported cleanly by new Kevlar/Mylar cloth laminates were

1980 America's Cup last race start / ROSS

all-round slightly better than Australia's. Denied the use of US-woven Kelvar/Mylar laminates by the New York Yacht Club, the Australians sourced a supply from the English cloth-maker Windmaster.

Race one was cut and dried in Freedom's favour after the Australians showed signs of stage fright on the first work and drifted behind on all legs in the 10-12 knot wind range until the last, when they picked up 35sec to finish 1min 52sec behind. A lay day followed, at Australia's request to gain another day's tuning with the new mast. The Dacron mainsail used in the first race looked powerful but was not completely happy in the roach area.

The first attempt to sail race two showed how potent Australia's rig could be in light weather. Again, she carried the Dacron main on the bent rig. She trailed Freedom around the first four marks and then on the run, with the wind fading right out from five knots, sailed around Freedom easily as both tacked downwind. Australia just reached the fifth mark when the time limit ran out with a full leg to sail, with Freedom wallowing 700 metres behind.

Australia, using her Kevlar/Mylar mainsail on the bent mast for the first time, was faster to windward in the race two re-sail, in six to eight knots of breeze. The lead changed four times with Australia finally winning by 28sec and beating the time limit by only 8min 18sec.

Race three could also have gone to Australia. She kept strong pressure on Freedom all the way in a 12-16 knot wind. Freedom's crew work cracked under the strain. Her spinnaker pole dropped in the water during a hoist, which could have developed into a serious gear breakdown and Australia only just missed taking the lead at the last mark rounding before Freedom went on to win by 53sec.

Race four, after a lay day called by Australia, went to Freedom by a comfortable 3min 48sec margin in a 12-16 knot wind when Australia wrongly selected her heavy weather mainsail set on a straightened mast for a 30-knot blow that never came. Freedom was too fast in the 14-17 knot winds of the

Above: 1980 last race, Freedom heads for win
Below: 1980 winner Freedom / ROSS

last race to lead around every mark and win by 3min 38sec.

Although Australia had gone into the America's Cup with a potent secret weapon, her crew was off balance, without complete confidence in what they had and this sometimes showed up on the race course. Freedom won every start except one. Ben Lexcen, who as tactician did a great job through the challenger eliminations, seemed to lose confidence and to be in awe of Conner and his tactician Dennis Durgan. He also had the burden of designing, building and tuning the bendy rig.

Freedom, helped by winning the starts, was adept at exploiting the wind shifts as well as covering Australia. She was helped in this by a component of her instrumentation that gave her true wind reading. Australia had the same Rochester instruments but could never get the true wind component to work properly. 'It was flown backwards and forwards so many times to the manufacturer in California, it got air-sick,' said Lexcen. 'I got tired towards the end; tried to do too much and stuffed up a couple of starts,' said Lexcen. 'If we had beaten the Swedes easily, instead of being held up by the breakages, we would have put that mast in before meeting the French.'

He said Australia's crew was still experimenting with sail trim in the Cup match. 'We only found the Kevlar/Mylar we could use in the last couple of weeks, from Windmaster, England. They had only just started making it so we ran out of time. The same old story, we have to start earlier. I didn't think the US sails were much different to ours. We were close on the sail shapes but I just think we didn't know really what sails to use when precisely enough because of our inaccurate testing. We didn't start using the boat properly until we got here. The new main meant the jibs had to be re-cut flatter. We didn't get around to all that.

'The crew in the America's Cup felt off balance. It might have been me.'

THE CREW THAT sailed Australia in the America's Cup match was: Skipper/helmsman Jim Hardy; tactician Ben Lexcen; navigator, Jack Baxter; mainsheet, Rob Brown; trimmers, John Bertrand, Skip Lissiman; grinders, Peter Costello and Phil Smidmore; pitman, John Longley; mastman, Peter Shipway; bow, Scott McAllister. Reserves: John Rosser, Joe Cooper, John Stanley and Jock Barker. Cooper sailed the last two races in place of Longley who injured his knee.

Lexcen said there was not much difference in the designs of the boats. 'Hull design was not the factor. They have just got their act together,' he said of Conner's campaign. 'We must get organised much sooner and in a way that the crew don't get bored to death. That is a big problem. I have a really low threshold of boredom where I don't do anything, just goof off all the time. I would rather have more things to do than have people take things off me.'

Grim as his situation may have been at times in Newport, Benny never missed an opportunity to raise a laugh. Australia's tender Fire III had a tape of the theme from Silvester Stallone's epic movie Rocky, not long before released. Sam Harris, Fire III's skipper, would play the tape in full stereophonic glory to fire up Australia's crew before the starts. Ben would respond by shadow boxing his way from stern to bow and back again for a few one-armed pushups on the after deck.

Alan Bond, despite the 1-4 scoreline, was jubilant. After the last race, he joined the crew aboard Australia on the tow back to Newport harbour and told them he had decided to challenge again in 1983 with a major effort in a new boat. Lexcen would design it, John Bertrand would be the skipper. Bond told the final press conference in Newport: 'It is the building of block upon block, brick upon brick that will eventually win this cup.' He turned to Jim Hardy and said: 'Jim, you have sailed Australia to the best of her ability. To Warren, Ben, they put together a yacht to the best of their ability of the technology in our country as it stands today. 1983 for me will be a new era because the New York Yacht Club has for the first time in the history of the club has seen the wisdom to change the rules to allow materials available worldwide to be used.'

Ben Lexcen told the press conference: 'I am so damn mad about losing this, but I will try again, maybe.' He added prophetically: 'I am sure there will be a big jump in technology in the boats over the next three years and I hope we can keep up with the jump.'

# 11

# DESIGNING
# AUSTRALIA II

D R PETER VAN OOSSANEN, WHO was head of design research
at the Netherlands Ship Model Basin, in 1981 persuaded the Bond
team to test Ben Lexcen's design ideas for the 1983 challenger Australia
II with large, one-third scale models, in the NSMB towing tank. Van
Oossanen had firm ties with Australia after spending 15 of his earli-
est years living there. His parents in 1951 joined the flow of European
migrants to Australia after World War Two when Peter was six years old.
They settled in the Sydney suburb of Mosman. Peter went to Mosman
Boys High School and then Balgowlah High School where he obtained
his leaving certificate. He sailed Moths from Balmoral Sailing Club
through that time.

He then did three years of the University of NSW naval architecture
course part time. Australia did not then have a full time naval architecture course at university level. Peter, who still speaks English with a
strong Australian accent, says: 'That was tedious, particularly as it wasn't

possible to find a job during the day in a design office or anything like that. At the end of 1963 – I'll never forget it – John Toft, a lecturer at the university, told us about this laboratory in The Netherlands where they had done a lot of research on the resistance of ships' propellers and stuff like that.'

Peter went home and asked his parents whether they realised that The Netherlands had a big tradition in naval architecture. His father (Piet senior) agreed, saying shipping was important to The Netherlands. Peter suggested going back to Holland to complete a naval architecture course. His parents decided that they should all go back as a family, at least for a holiday, in 1964 to have a look at The Netherlands and see if it had changed much.

Peter, who was then 21, enrolled at Delft University and gained his degree in naval architecture. He met his wife Dina, who didn't feel like moving to Australia after he finished his education. His parents also decided to stay in The Netherlands. 'It had been difficult for them to go to Australia in first place,' said Peter. 'Like many migrants, they found it tough being removed from their family ties. But my younger brother Robert, as soon as he was 18, went back to Australia all by himself. He was almost born in Australia and was as much Australian as you can get.'

PETER AFTER FINISHING his studies joined the staff of the Netherlands Ship Model Basin at Wageningen, a small city (population 33,000) near the German border. The inland site was chosen because it offered rock foundations for the large towing tanks, not to be found in the low-lying lands nearer the sea. The facility, founded by the Dutch government and industry in 1929, offered much more than the original deep-water towing tank. A whole series of special test laboratories was successively built to cope with the ever-increasing demands of the shipping industry for research into powering performance, sea keeping and manoeuvring. The NSMB has since been re-named The Maritime Research Institute (MARIN) to better reflect its functions. It employs about 300 people and has an annual turnover of 33 million euros, 85 per cent of that in the commercial worldwide maritime market.

The NSMB offered many more research opportunities to Ben Lexcen than the New York Yacht Club envisaged when it gave Alan Bond's team permission to test large scale models there because there were no facilities for testing models of that scale in Australia. It also exposed him to new, creative ideas from scientists and researchers in fields far beyond conventional yacht design.

Up to that time in America's Cup history, designers had never totally trusted the results of towing tank testing over their own calculations and intuition. The Bond syndicate's exclusive deal with the NSMB was to give it a huge, unforeseen advantage in its 1983 America's Cup campaign.

In the late 1970s, van Oossanen, because of his Australian background, was visiting Australia regularly to consult with the tank's customers there. 'That's when my interests in sailing boats really revived,' he says. 'And I remember the first time Alan Bond's Australia was campaigning; designed by Ben together with Johan Valentijn ... I wrote a letter to Alan Bond in 1978 suggesting that they do research at the towing tank with big-scale models. I was convinced that was the way to go. They had been testing at Delft University, which has a small tank and the models employed were tiny.

'I got a letter back from Warren Jones after a few weeks. He said that the budget for 1980 was insufficient to do anything of that nature but they would consider that option later. He said to me, 'Why don't you meet up with Ben in Sydney and maybe discuss a few things'. And so, Warren organised a meeting and I met Ben for the first time; that was in 1978. He took me to his home in Seaforth and we looked at lines plans and we discussed keels and rudders, we discussed sail plans, we discussed everything. We met on a Saturday and we were together the whole weekend. We went to Pittwater to have a look at some of the boats; he was interested in Six Metres and 5.5s at the time as well. We discussed bustles and skegs and all that sort of thing. So, it was quite a good first acquaintance and we got along well.

'I didn't hear anything more from him for two years. I followed their progress in the 1980 campaign with the bendy mast when they won one race but didn't do well. I had worked out that they lost out on most of the upwind legs.

'But then out of the blue I got a phone call from Ben; he said, 'I'm on my way to Holland; I would like to visit you and visit the tank tomorrow!'

'He rang me on a Friday. I said, 'Hang on tomorrow is Saturday.'

'And he said, 'Is that a problem?'

'Not really.'

'So, I got the keys to the whole towing tank place and when Ben dropped in on Saturday morning; he'd travelled down from Amsterdam. We went through the tanks and I remember he was absolutely thrilled. It's just a massive place with so many facilities. [At that time, the institute had five towing tanks, three cavitation tunnels and a huge computer department.]

'He said to me. 'Alright, you've convinced me that big models are the way to go because you are looking at small differences between 12 metres. The nature of the America's Cup is all about small differences.' 'I was convinced that you could only pick up small differences by using very, very big models. So, I suggested one-to-three scale models. Those models themselves would weigh 950kg; you're talking about a small boat like a 5.5 or a Six Metre almost. He said to me, 'Can you make a proposal for a total R and D campaign.' That's what I did. I had to address it to Warren Jones. And within two weeks or so they approved my proposal.'

The Bond syndicate secured an exclusive deal to use the NSMB's services initially for about 125,000 Dutch guilders (about 50,000 Euros). That was later approximately doubled when additional testing was required to evaluate the performance of the winged keel. Van Oossanen travelled to Sydney and met Lexcen and Warren Jones to discuss details of the work to be done. He received lines plans and other technical data from Lexcen.

Van Oossanen proposed two programs. The first was to test a model of the existing Australia hull shape with its existing keel and with a similar thicker keel housing more ballast lower down, designed by Lexcen. 'The proposal basically consisted of two parts. One part was to do a test of the existing Australia hull shape. And Ben said he some ideas about a thicker keel that would have more lead and more stability.

The second approach was to have The Netherlands Aerospace Laboratory in Amsterdam, as a sub-contractor, do CFD (Computational Fluid Dynamic) calculations on a number of different keel shapes. 'I proposed that we do some very radical keel shapes, including an upside-down keel, with a wider chord at the bottom than the top,' said van Oossanen. 'I remember Ben didn't think much of that approach but he said, 'Alright if you think that is maybe a way to discover some remaining options in the design rule, that's what we should do.''

The model of the Australia hull, with the original keel, was ready to go into the tank when Ben and Yvonne arrived in Wageningen on April 28, 1981. Lexcen was to spend four months there. He had his own office and typically consulted with van Oossanen from four o'clock each afternoon on research progress and developments.

Lexcen, initially following the philosophy of small differences gaining the edge under the Twelve Metre rule, developed the conventional boat to the stage where he was preparing its construction drawings. That boat, with the same waterline length, canoe body shape and displacement as Australia, ultimately became Challenge 12, the boat the Bond team later decided to build in parallel to Australia II as insurance in case the winged keel, short canoe body concept, did not perform as the tank predicted.

Van Oossanen was left to work on the radical program, because he already had the contacts with the aerospace laboratory. Initially, Lexcen was sceptical of this approach. 'He would always attend the meetings and looked at the results of what the calculations were showing, but maybe because he couldn't understand part of all that, because it was a very scientific exercise; or because he didn't believe in the results or didn't give them much of a priority, he wasn't interested that much.'

He did become keenly interested when Joop Slooff, the scientist in charge of the department at the aerospace laboratory where the CFD testing was being carried out, reported that the upside-down keel was looking particularly good in the computer. 'Then we had quite a few sessions with Ben about why would the upside-down keel concept be any better than a normal, traditional keel,' said van Oossanen. 'We pinpointed the fact that the centre of side force is lower down from the water surface so that the disturbance the side force pressure distribution would cause in the way of additional wave drag would be less. Maybe that was something he could visualise.'

Slooff, who had previously reporting progress of the NLR research by telephone, visited the NSMB to meet van Oossanen and Lexcen with the detailed results of computer research in on May 19, 1981. He suggested that a model should be made to test the quite promising results.

The major disadvantage of the upside-down keel was the enormous tip vortex at its bottom. To overcome that, Slooff suggested looking at end plates or winglets, which were already being used by aeroplane designers. Lexcen was already well aware of tip vortex problems from his offshore designs and to reduce them had experimented with end plates on his 18ft skiff and 5.5 metre class designs.

Slooff suggested a further analysis by NLR's CFD program with a set of crude winglets on the present model, at little extra cost, to which Lexcen and Warren Jones agreed. Two weeks after their approval, Slooff telephoned Van Oossanen and said, 'You won't believe this but the upside-down keel with the winglets is yielding something like 25 per cent more side force, 20 per cent less keel drag and the results are just too good to be true.'

Van Oossanen said: 'When I had that phone call I went over to Ben's office and said, 'Ben, you won't believe this but this is what these guys are saying.'

'And I remember Ben, saying, 'Fuck! Do you really think this is true?"

'And I said, 'Well I had great respect for Joop Slooff and the aerospace laboratory. We had done work with them before. These are serious people; these people are at the forefront of aerodynamics and aeroplane development and if this is what they are reporting there's a 99 per cent chance that it's true.'

'And Ben, said, 'Okay I've going to call Warren because we've got to test this in the tank; there is no way we can just bank on these calculations."

Both Lexcen and van Oossanen then consulted Warren Jones by telephone. Jones who was managing director of America's Cup Challenge 1983 Ltd, the company formed by Alan Bond to support his 1983 challenge, said: 'If I can convince Alan, the money can be made available and then maybe you should start as quickly as possible because this is going to have a major effect on our planning.'

Jones had given Lexcen a strict deadline to the time that Steve Ward had to begin building the boat in Perth. Bond gave his approval within 24 hours. Lexcen by now was excited by the winged-keel concept, which he called 'Darth Vader'. An avid movie-goer, he saw its similarity to the helmet worn by that space-odyssey character in Star Wars. In a telex message to Warren Jones on May 22, 1981, Lexcen in an unmistakeably characteristic code, said:

NEED TO CONVERSE ON DOG AND BONE WITH MISSION
IMPOSSIBLE HEAD OF OZ.
SICK OF CHEESE AND BREAD.
KEEL III A BIG ADVANCE.
ABOUT TO TAKE YACHT DESIGN INTO SPACE AGE.
DARTH VADER LOOKS GOOD IN COMPUTER IN 3
DIMENSION
WILL TEST ON WEDNESDAY 10TH JUNE. CAN'T RETURN
TO LAND OF OZ UNTIL 17TH JUNE. NEED BRASS AND
CONVERSATION.
LLOYDS COMING UNDER CONTROL.
BEN SKYWALKER.

Van Oossanen explained that Lexcen was homesick, looking forward to escaping the rain of The Netherlands for the sunshine of Australia and that he always had problems with Lloyds, the measurement authority, because he wanted to do structures that Lloyds wouldn't approve.

The model with crude plate-like winglets on the upside-keel was tested in the towing tank on June 9 and 10. Coincidentally, Joop Slooff arrived at the tank on June 10 with detailed results of the NLR computer research. 'So, we went to the tank and had a look at some of the initial tank results and they were very, very promising,' van Oossanen recalled.

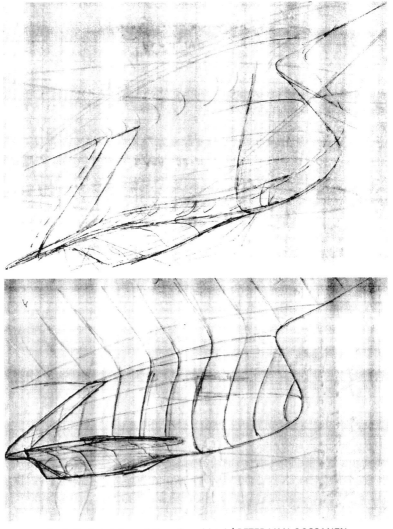

Ben's first sketches of the winged keel / PETER VAN OOSSANEN

'We went to a meeting room with Ben there. Basically, the results Joop Slooff had on paper were pretty close to what we had been getting from the tank. We were actually talking like 25 per cent more side force and 20 per cent less drag on that particular keel.'

While they were talking, Lexcen sketched the winged-keel concept showing how he visualised the winglets becoming a streamlined integral part of the keel – as they eventually were in Australia II's keel.

'THIS IS HOW he visualised the keel. It wasn't looking like this at that stage. The upside-down keel was there, the trim tab was there, but the winglets we had at that stage were like extraneous add-ons and this was like an integrated design.

'This again pinpoints Ben's unique ability to visualise something in his mind and then to put it on paper very, very quickly with just a few strokes of his pencil,' said Van Oossanen. 'I hadn't come across anyone who could do that. He had a great respect for ... someone like me, someone who knew his mathematics, knew his science and could explain why the water did that and not something else. And I think that's why we had such a good relationship because I didn't, and still don't have, the knack of being able to visualise how something is going to look like and actually sketch it out and have that flair for having seen a shape and being able to reproduce it like he did.'

Van Oossanen on analysing the tank results found that the since the side-force resistance had been increased by more than 40 per cent, the keel could be much smaller and then, with the permission of Lexcen and Jones, prepared and tested a much smaller keel/winglet model. He says that this became the final keel and winglets, which Lexcen approved before travelling to Australia on June 20. Lexcen, by now thoroughly convinced that his team had a design breakthrough, had decided to return to Australia to talk about strategy with Jones and Bond. Should one or two boats be built? How could the wing-keeled hull be kept secret?

Van Oossanen, after further testing of the model with the smaller keel and winglets and comparing all the calculations and predictions with those for the Twelve that was to become Challenge 12, concluded that the wetted surface of the whole Australia II concept was still too large. And because there was more lead in the keel lower down providing greater stability, under the Twelve Metre Rule, a smaller boat with a 44ft waterline carrying a larger sail area could be designed. After consulting Lexcen in Sydney with details by mail and telex, van Oossanen and his staff drew a new lines plan, retaining the forebody and removing a significant part of the bustle, making it more vee-shaped, to obtain a smaller displacement and the associated reduction in wetted area.

With time running out before the builder's deadline, Warren Jones asked van Oossanen to fly to Sydney as soon as possible to inform Lexcen of the details. Van Oossanen arrived in Sydney on July 15. After discussing the plans and concept, Lexcen elected to re-draw the bustle, which he did over the weekend of July 18-19. Van Oossanen flew back to The Netherlands to test this configuration in the tank with the newly-designed keel and winglets. He said: 'The final test (on August 6) with the altered canoe body and the final keel and winglets proved to yield the finally-designed performance, with excellent properties in light conditions (for the months of June, July and August in Newport) and in moderate to high wind speeds sailing upwind (September).

'I informed Ben of the results on August 7, 1981. He requested full-scale offsets, hydrostatic calculations, performance predictions, mast location, 1-10 scale lines plan, photographs, etc. I then provided full-scale loftings to Ben for building the mould for the keel and winglets (which I saw being built during my next visit to Sydney) and loftings (provided in the form of a table of offsets) for the new hull, which I sent to Perth. Ben then assisted the builder (Steve Ward) in Perth in drawing a full-scale body plan on the loft floor.'

The involvement of the Dutch researchers and scientists in Australia II's design was later to be questioned in the prolonged dispute over the legality of Australia II's keel generated by the US defender syndicate during the 1983 Cup campaigning in Newport. The America's Cup Deed of Gift is vague on its country-of-origin rule, which reads ... 'the designers of the yacht's hull, rig and sails shall be nationals of that country ...'

The NYCC, in qualifying its permission to allow the Bond syndicate to use the NSMB facility, said: 'Officially your tank tests in the Netherlands Ship Model Basin are entirely within the rules if: (1) They were under the sole supervision of Australian nationals; (2) The designs were from the drawing board of Australian nationals; and (3) The results are used in the design of that Australian challenger only.'

While the Dutch scientists did contribute significant ideas, Lexcen had supervised the whole design process step-by-step, made the decisions including adopting the upside-down keel and produced the final lines plan. With the keel, he was responsible for the jump between the crude add-on winglets to the integrated wings of the final design. He designed the structure, the sail plan, the rig and the rudder.

During the final processes of the Australia II design, Alan Bond, Warren Jones and John Bertrand visited the NSMB to check on its progress. Bertrand had been skippering Bond's Apollo II in the Admiral's Cup international offshore teams racing championship at Cowes and they flew into Wageningen by helicopter on the lay day. Van Oossanen gave a full account of the work that had been carried out in a meeting that Joop Slooff also attended. 'I went through it all in about two and a-half hours. After I had finished, Warren was quite pleased and Alan was very thrilled.

'And then John Bertrand said: 'This is all bullshit. I don't believe any of this and I have a fluid mechanics degree. I don't believe that this sort of jump in performance can be obtained, particularly by something that looks like that. I'm going to be looking a fool if I am going to be steering a boat like this.'

'Warren then said, 'Well hang on John, you haven't heard what we really want to do.'

'And then he said, and this was news for me as well, 'Look, we'll do two boats. We'll build Ben's fat keel boat and we'll build this one and we will sail them side by side."

The Bond team had been negotiating with potential syndicates in Queensland and Victoria to take over the conventional boat. 'We'll call those deals off. We'll build both boats and maybe if one of the two boats doesn't quite work out, later on we can always sell it.'

'That's when John sort of shut up,' said van Oossanen.

# 12

# 'DARTH VADER' IN AUSTRALIA

Back in Western Australia, first insights of Australia II's design drew astonishment among the Bond's team leadership, among them John Longley who project managed the Australia II campaign from January 1981 until executive director Warren Jones took over the role in 1983 to allow Longley to focus on crewing aboard the boat.

'Benny was in Holland tank-testing and he suddenly stopped talking about the new yacht but the boat with the Darth Vader keel,' Longley recalled. 'In those early days, very few of us in Western Australia knew what was happening in Holland; Alan obviously, Warren and myself. And the bizarre picture was slowly building in our minds of this weird and wonderful boat.'

When Longley went to see Steve Ward, who had built Australia for the 1977 America's Cup and modified her for 1980 and showed him the basic plans for Australia II, Steve said: 'Hey, Benny's flipped this time.'

Next concern was keeping the design and especially the upside-down winged keel, a secret for 13 months while the boat was built and sailed in Fremantle and Melbourne before being shipped to Newport for the Cup campaign. I remember when we first started building the boat having to go and talk to the engineers at the State Engineering Works who had cast the keel,' said Longley. 'It was one thing to design it; the other thing was to make it. And to go down there and speak to a large government organisation and say, 'You have to build something that is 17 to 18 tonnes and is three dimensional'. Imagine the infrastructure for making a pattern of that and casting that and no-one around the place is to know anything about it. And there was this amazing fact that we cast that keel in North Fremantle and we built the boat in Cottesloe and no-one ever really found out about it.'

Steve Ward's team began building the boat in aluminium on November 2, 1981 for the Bond syndicate, which was officially named America's Cup Challenge 1983 Ltd and again challenging through the Royal Perth Yacht Club.

Lexcen later in November returned from a trip around the world during which, in England, he discussed with Lloyds and boat-builder Jeremy Rogers the possibility of having him build the Bond syndicate's second Twelve in fibreglass. Lexcen also consulted Lewmar winches, re-visited the NSMB in Holland and in the USA looked at various mast extrusions, spoke to instrument and on-board computer

Australia II and Challenge 12, Westpac series, January 1983 / ROSS

Challenge 12 and Australia II, Westpac series / ROSS

manufacturers and checked the onshore facilities in Newport.

The second 'conventional' Lexcen design, which became Challenge 12, was, however, eventually built in aluminium by Ward for a Melbourne syndicate challenging through the Royal Yacht Club of Victoria, with construction beginning in March 1982. The Bond syndicate had readily agreed to sell the design and help the Victorians put together an aggressive training partner aiming to become the America's Cup challenger in its own right. If Challenge 12 proved to be faster than Australia II, the Bond syndicate would still have time to build a similar Twelve in aluminium in time to ship to Newport in April 1983.

When Australia II was launched in June 1982 at Success Harbour, Fremantle, Alan Bond spoke of a 'secret weapon'. Elaborate precautions were taken to conceal her underwater shape and appendage. The keel and all the under body from the rudder post to the bow overhang were shrouded by tarpaulins. After launching the yacht, with the bottom antifouled, was kept in the water instead of being hauled out on the hydraulic lift available at Success Harbour. The tarpaulins at the launching fell apart far enough at the stern to suggest that the hull had very little bustle ahead of a small rudder. Best guess by outsiders of the keel shape at that time was that it was a fin-bulb style. A clever paint scheme effectively camouflaged the upside-down configuration of the keel from observers and photographers on the water and in the air.

Australia II showed her incredible manoeuvrability the short waterline and small keel gave her that was to be so effective in the America's

Cup, on her very first sail. John Longley recalled: 'We had terrible problems getting the sails up. We had no idea whether this boat was going to act like a yacht. I sashayed up to the bow and John Bertrand said, 'Let's see whether or not we can tack this thing.'

'And he threw the helm down as you would on any Twelve Metre. I was holding onto the forestay. This was my fourth America's Cup challenge so I knew what was likely to happen and I almost went in because no one had expected what then happened, although that became one of the great assets of the boat, the incredible manoeuvrability; the boat just flicked around.

'And John Bertrand said straight away, 'We are never going to do that again until we get to Newport. We have always got to tack this boat as if it is a normal boat.''

Australia II sailed through winter from Fremantle, with three intense periods to try out potential crew members from the eastern states. The boat was not quite right, floating slightly down by the stern and feeling out of trim to Bertrand. Lexcen had positioned the keel nine inches too far aft. The correcting alteration was made at Yanchep, away from prying eyes. In getting there from Fremantle, the relatively light Australia II showed the ability to surf readily. 'The day we left to go up to Yanchep it was blowing about a 35-knot nor'-wester, so we turned back,' said Longley. 'The next day was an absolutely gorgeous day; not a breath of wind. We fired up Black Swan (Australia II's tender) and we roared up to Yanchep. We got to the reefs; there are two lines of reefs, the eight-mile reef and the four-mile reef. We got to the eight-mile reef and sat off there a bit, figuring out a good break in the waves and just going for it. We sat off for about half an hour and we watched until we figured out where they were breaking.

'We went for it with myself and one other bloke on the 12. Everything was going fine and suddenly dear old Phil Judge came up in his most laconic manner and said: 'Hey Chink, don't look behind you now.' I turned around and there was this classic Hawaii Five O wave behind us. Suddenly the flat spot in front disappeared and all I could see was the tow line going into the back of this wave and suddenly she was off.

'We surfed straight over the reef with water creaming out either side and Phil came up and said, 'She surfs pretty good, Chink.''

Meantime, the Melbourne syndicate was having difficulty raising funds. It had appointed key crew members: former Etchells world champion John Savage as helmsman, offshore big boat sailor Graeme

Freeman as project manager and Col Anderson, of the Hood loft in Melbourne, as chief sailmaker. Savage went to Fremantle in July for helming practice aboard Australia II.

The launching of Challenge 12 was delayed a month while the Victorian syndicate was unable to come up with the money to pay the builder Ward, designer Lexcen and mast-maker Zapspar. Finally, the Bond syndicate, anxious to get the co-operative training program under way, made a charter arrangement with the Victorians to get Challenge 12 sailing. The delay helped rather than hindered the Challenge 12 program with the boat completely race ready when she was launched on November 23. Australia II was alongside her in Steve Ward's Cottesloe shed, having a further modification to the keel. So, Challenge 12's project manager Freeman could step across to Australia II, which had an identical deck layout, winching system and hydraulics to consult her project manager Longley.

In the first ten days of intensive training, through hours of straight-line tuning and the first match-racing brushes, the boats looked to be evenly matched with success often depending on sail selection. The two boats had identical sail plans and the sails were swapped between them. One day they sailed 28 miles together in two long legs way out beyond Rottnest Island before Australia II could gain a two boat-length advantage.

In the racing, Australia II held the edge, winning all but one race, in which she lost the lead by crewing error, but only by small margins. And that could have been accounted for by the greater experience of the Australia II crew in Twelve Metre racing. The Victorians felt that downwind, in under 13 knots of true wind and a 'joggly' sea, that their heavier conventional boat was faster and had the ability to sail lower on the runs. Both crews agreed that having two brand-new well-matched sophisticated Twelves racing against each other was a luxury that Australia had never before enjoyed in preparing for the America's Cup. John Bertrand said that more was learned in the first weekend of sailing against Challenge 12 than in all the time Australia spent sailing alone on home waters before the 1980 challenge.

The Victorian syndicate, however, was still unable to find the corporate support it needed to pay off the earlier bills and the charter fee. A crisis was reached on January 26, 1983, when Bond announced that as a result, his syndicate would take over Challenge 12's sailing program. Within a few days the philanthropic Melbourne businessman Dick Pratt, who had already given $100,000, within a few days stepped in to pay out

Downwind duel, Australia II and Challenge 12, Westpac series / ROSS

$300,000 of the amount owed the Bond syndicate to retain Challenge 12 and take over leadership of the syndicate. He was probably the first syndicate head in the history of the America's Cup to admit that he had never stepped aboard a yacht!

Pratt quickly revived the Challenge 12 crew's preparation program, with new sails and a new mast added to the two they already had. In five weeks, after working 12-hour days for seven days a week at sea and on shore, Challenge 12 was fully competitive with Australia II in the West-pac Advance Australia Cup series, sailed on Port Phillip from the Royal Yacht Club of Victoria in March. Joining Australia II and Challenge 12 for the Westpac series was Gretel II, the 1970 and 1977 Alan-Payne designed challenger owned by Gordon Ingate, which had been serving as a trial horse in Sydney for the new challenger Advance, designed by Payne for Syd Fischer, which did not contest the Westpac series because she was behind in her preparation program.

The Bond syndicate established a Newport-style situation for the Westpac series and the training that preceded it from January with living quarters and administration offices in the old Customs House next to the RYCV in Williamstown. The RYCV installed a travel lift and improved its hard-standing area to accommodate the Twelves. The Challenge 12 crew also had a live-in situation at a nearby Army base.

The 13-race series showed that there was little between Australia II and Challenge 12 in performance. Australia II was obviously a very stiff boat upwind, helped by the concentration of weight low down in the keel. Challenge 12 at times was faster downwind. Australia II did show on the start line, once or twice, the incredible ability to spin around in her own length that Bertrand had vowed to keep secret.

Each boat beat the other twice, with human error the deciding factor, before Australia II won the final by 3min 34sec after Challenge 12 lost time with a broken headsail halyard at the start of the last beat. Gretel II won only one race, against Challenge 12, which was disqualified when she failed to return to re-start after being over the line early. But she was beaten over the half-size (12.2n mile) America's Cup style courses by three to four minutes in most races, dispelling Ben Lexcen's recurring nightmare that both his boats might be slow. The event was an important springboard for both Australia II and Challenge 12 before they were shipped to Newport in April. Bertrand said at the end of the series: 'We are light years ahead of previous Australian challenges at this stage.'

Executive director of the Bond syndicate, Warren Jones, said the day after the Westpac series: 'We close ranks once we have selected our team. We don't let anybody in and we don't let anybody out. So, we always keep our complete unit, or 'wedge' as we call it, fully informed as to

The Twelves base at the Royal Yacht Club of Victoria,
Williamstown, for the Westpac series / ROSS

what we are doing to achieve the bench marks we have set with regards to boat efficiency, crew work, target dates.

'Through our Fremantle training period we set out to get the boat to the stage where, when she came to Victoria, nothing had to be done to her structurally. Victoria was a stage of simulating Newport where we could go to a crew house, pick our team and do what we do in Newport. And that has worked very well; it gave us the opportunity to observe the guys and make sure we selected people who were homogenous. A lot of other teams have broken down in Newport because of having different personalities trying to live in an intense situation with each other for four months. So, we have been through that phase here.'

What did Ben Lexcen think?

The day after the Westpac series I am sitting below in the 'sewer' of Australia II and feeling distinctly nervous. I am trying for the fourth day in a row to interview Ben Lexcen, on what he thinks of the form of his two new Twelves in the Westpac series. Australia II the previous day won the final race of the series over a full 24.5n mile America's Cup course. In their four meetings during the previous heats over half-size America's Cup courses the score was two-all. I am keen to get Ben's reaction to the result.

At last I have cornered the mercurial Benny but he is pre-occupied with a peculiar problem. The hydraulic ram that tensions Australia II's rig by lifting the mast step has blown a seal, leaving the mast jammed in the fully-tensioned position. The mast must come out so that the boat can be packed up for the USA. There is no way of reaching the faulty ram which is enclosed in the mast. Ben with some temporary hydraulic jacks is trying to lift an edge of the mast far enough to remove blocks supporting it. While support-group member Steve Harrison pushes and pulls at the runners and deck-level mast ram to rock the bottom of the mast, Ben belts away at the blocks with a hammer.

Somehow it seems to be the wrong time to be questioning him about the sophisticated design and engineering features – including a revolutionary and still secret keel – of what has been hailed as the most potent and best-prepared challenger of all time. But as Ben hammers, I persist. How did he feel about the outcome of the Westpac series? 'It confirms my confidence in this boat but the other one is better than I thought it would be.'

When would he show the world the tricky keel? 'We are even going to hide it in America, keep a bag around it to keep the opposition worrying about it. You see, even if they knew what it is like, they wouldn't know if we had changed it.'

In performance terms, what was it doing for the boat? 'The boat goes faster, it does not go sideways as much; it allows the boat to sail more upright.'

*More hammering. 'Have you got the bigger jack, Steve? Shoot it down here.'*

It does seem you are the only designer with something different. 'The other guys have tried different things haven't they and they have not been able to get them to work. We might have it working; we don't know.'

Gordon Ingate, owner-skipper of Gretel II joins us. He is an engineer and marvels at what Ben is trying to do. Jokingly, he offers to lend Ben some bolt cutters to snip a shroud and relieve the tension on the rig.

Ben: 'Who would cut it? Who would be game enough to? Where would you end up when it went? Whooo... the mast would end up over the other side of the shipyard and the bloke the other side of the car park somewhere.'

By now Steve has pushed the mast all the way forward with the deck-level ram and loaded the runners to the point that the mast, through the open hatch above us, looks like an archer's bow just before the arrow is loosed. Ben tells us there is 57,000 lb of tension on the rigging. 'There is more load on the mast right now than the weight of the boat. The rig has stretched three inches.'

Lexcen says he is thankful that Gretel II, the promising challenger of 1970 and campaigned again in 1977, had competed in Melbourne. 'Before Gordon came down here I was really depressed, starting to get second thoughts; maybe I'm mad maybe they're both a couple of dogs. Gordon did pretty good. They are not dogs, they are in the right area. Maybe they're better, maybe they're worse.

'I know from our tests that Challenge 12 is faster than our old boat (Australia, 1980 challenger). It is faster upwind in light weather but only microscopically, 10sec on a beat. But in a breeze that boat is much faster than our old boat. Its righting moment is heaps up on the old boat.' He adds that Australia II is probably another 10 per cent stiffer than Challenge 12.

Ingate remarks that Challenge 12 had passed Australia II downwind. Ben comments: 'It's spinnakers. In the tank, this boat has exactly the same drag and that is the most reliable thing in the tank that you can do. On the wind, this one is definitely better; there is no doubt of it in my mind. It has the manoeuvrability aspect, which is a big plus if you can use it right. The tacking and acceleration of this boat is superior.'

Ingate: 'We did three tacks with them and they gained a minute.'

Lexcen: 'Acceleration is like a rocket.'

*More hammering and the whole boat groans. Ben to Steve: 'Yeah, the mast's right forward; just let the runners off and pump the forestay down as far as it will go. I think we will get it out Steve.'*

I exchange glances with Ingate and sense that he, too, is looking for a decent excuse to leave. But I stay. This is only time Ben has been in one spot for more than five minutes in a week.

What is the displacement of Australia II? 'I'm not telling you. It is lightish and the boat is fairly long. This boat has long sailing length and short waterline and so is a light boat. We have no bustle and a dinghy rudder. It feels like a dinghy to sail too. It does not feel like a Twelve Metre it has the responses of a dinghy. If you pull it away, it accelerates straight away.'

Ingate: 'Do you see what Alan Payne is getting at with Advance?'

'No, it is just bloody odd. I think he has tried to make the hull generate side force. I don't think that's the way to go when you can make keels so efficient.

'We did (theoretical) tests, segmenting the boat into three sections. The front of the boat has something like 10 per cent of the lift. The mid-

Left: Benny tries on new shoes from a team sponsor. Right top: Leaps for joy. Right: John Bertrand at the shoe handout says, 'Come on guys, let's go sailing' ROSS

dle of the boat where the keel is, like 90 per cent and the back of the boat where the bustle has negative lift. It pushes the boat to leeward. That's why I took the bustle off.'

*'A-frame coming aft, forestay off first.' The boat groans a loud sigh of relief in a key that Lexcen says is A-flat.*

He tries to re-assure us. 'I put safety factors like one and a-half and two into critical things like chainplates and things low down where the weight doesn't count and up high I put minus safety factors.'

*'Has the mast come aft?'*

*'Not enough to get it off this thing, I can tell you that.'*

*'Can you rake it some more?'*

*'Is that ram right out and pull the runners on a bit'*

Lexcen, hammering at the block: 'I'll get this out if I get the f...ing Nobel Peace prize for engineering in pieces.'

'BANG!' One of the minus safety factors has had enough. The adjustment thread on a spreader base breaks. With a tremendous bang that has shell-shocked Twelve Metre crewmen all over the dockside area ducking for cover, the rig frees itself from the torturing hydraulics. There is relief all round. 'Good,' says Lexcen. 'Now we can get the mast out.' The crew is pleased because they now cannot take part in a public-relations sail-past of the boats along the St Kilda foreshore. I am pleased just to be able to walk away.

# 13

# KEELGATE

WHILE THE AUSTRALIA II TEAM packed up for Newport with confidence from three previous America's Cup campaign and excitement in the potential of the newest Ben Lexcen creation, the US defence candidates remained near-stalled in design development. The strongest group, the Fort Schuyler Maritime Academy again backing the 1980 winner Dennis Conner, aware that Ben Lexcen would explore radical ideas after his parting prediction of a leap in technology in Twelve Metres after Freedom's win that year, also looked to the corners of the design rule.

It had Johan Valentijn, the collaborator with Lexcen on the 1977 and 1980 challenger Australia, explore the possibility of a small, lightweight boat with Magic, while Sparkman & Stephens looked to the deep and heavy end of the rule with Spirit. Magic at 45,000 lb (20,412kg) was even lighter than Australia II (52,000 lb, 23,587kg) and highly manoeuvrable; Spirit was faster than Magic in straight line sailing. But in testing through the northern hemisphere summer of 1982, neither could match Freedom.

So, the syndicate asked Valentijn to design another yacht combining the best features of all three boats. The New York Yacht Club chose this yacht, Liberty, as its America's Cup defender after trials against the new Dave Pedrick design Defender, skippered by Tom Blackaller and the seven-year-old Courageous (John Kolius), the 1974 America's Cup winner, both supported by the same syndicate headed by well-known ocean racer Chuck Kirsch.

Liberty, said Conner, was very similar to Freedom at the top and bottom of the wind speed range but had a measurable speed advantage in the mid-range of conditions. However, the US defender trials did not have the same intensity of those in the previous two America's Cup campaigns and as they proceeded, Australia II was showing her potential in the Louis Vuitton Cup challenger elimination series. Conner had one of his team members watching the challenger trials almost every day from a support boat and came to realise Liberty would have a real fight on her hands in the America's Cup. 'While we had predicted that there would be a fast foreign boat in 1983, I know that I never imagined she could be THAT fast,' he said. 'Challenge 12 was about what we expected the Australian team to come up with.'

Equally obvious to Australia II's speed and incredible manoeuvrability was the professionally-settled nature of her crew and support team, many of them into their fourth Bond syndicate America's Cup campaign and the strength of its leadership under Warren Jones, who said reflectively on the tenth anniversary of Australia II's America's Cup win: 'We learned a tremendous amount in 1977 and were good enough to beat all the other challengers. In 1980, we were getting better at picking the right people; we should have won the America's Cup. By 1983 we had a unique combination of people and Benny Lexcen had given us the tools and above all of that, we believed in ourselves. Through the campaign we showed the benefits of a strong shore base and a strong sea base. And we cared for each other and kept caring.'

The New York Yacht Club was worried too as Australia II showed she was clearly faster in the first two round robins of the Louis Vuitton Cup against challengers from Great Britain (Victory '83), Italy (Azzurra), Canada (Canada 1), France (France 3) as well as the other two Australian challengers, Challenge 12 and Advance.

On July 24, when Australia II had accumulated a 15-win to two-loss

Makeshift wings being fitted to Freedom's keel / ROSS

record into Round Robin series B of the Louis Vuitton Cup, the Freedom/Liberty syndicate and the America's Cup committee of the New York Yacht Club opened what was to be a month-long sustained assault on the legality of Australia II's winged keel. The committee's chairman Robert McCullough wrote to Mark Vinbury, the New York Yacht Club's representative on the international measurement committee in Newport with Australian Jack Savage representing the Challenger of Record, the Royal Sydney Yacht Squadron and the International Yacht Racing Union's chief measurer Tony Watts (Great Britain), who was chairman, questioning whether Australia II had been 'fairly rated under the rating rule and measurement instructions of the International Twelve Metre Class in view of the wing-like appendages which extend outward and downward from the bottom of her keel'.

The international measurement committee had already measured Australia II and unanimously endorsed her as a Twelve Metre. She had first been measured in Australia in March by the IYRU-appointed measurer Ken McAlpine and had a rating certificate signed by the Australian Yachting Federation.

The NYYC's America's Cup committee argued that the winged keel was a 'peculiarity', which under Rule 27 of the Twelve Metre rating rule would not rate the yacht fairly and that she gained unmeasured draft when heeled. The committee pushed that argument, strongly supported by American designers Britton Chance and Halsey Herreshoff, who more than coincidentally was Liberty's navigator, through the US Yacht Racing Union to the keelboat technical committee of the IYRU.

Later – too late as it eventuated – the NYYC America's Cup committee questioned whether Lexcen had in fact designed the keel and hull or whether they had been the product of The Netherlands Aerospace Laboratory and Netherlands Ship Model Basin, in contravention of the Cup condition that all competing yachts must be 'designed by nationals of the country for which they compete'.

Warren Jones held his fire and with chess-player aplomb countered the NYYC's every move, shrewdly using the media pack in Newport baying for news, to his advantage. He would stop his bicycle at any Australian journalist he trusted and drop a bait: 'We've heard their latest move is .... See what you can suss out.'

Jones delivered a double-barrelled salvo on August 13 in a press release to the media pack that invoked the name of the successful and revered American designer Olin Stephens: 'Since Australia II first demonstrated her worthiness as a serious challenger for the America's Cup, we have been consistently and improperly badgered by false accusations concerning Australia II's keel design and rating.

'It was most pleasing when, at the International 12 Metre Association meeting this week, the most respected authority on 12 M concepts Olin Stephens said that he would hate to see Australia II removed from competition merely because she was fast.'

Jones in the same press release rolled out the hand grenade he had tucked away since he received it on July 27; a telex from Ed Du Moulin, manager of the Freedom campaign, asking Dr Van Oossanen of the Netherlands Ship Model Basin permission to build an Australia II keel for one of its boats, which was really an obvious ploy to flush out the nationality issue: 'Understand that you and your team are responsible for the development of special keel for Australia II. We are finally convinced of her potential and would therefore like to build same design under one of our boats.

'We will keep this confidential as not to jeopardise your agreement with Alan Bond however due to complexity of problems, need your maximum input and experience. We can start next week and be ready by August 25. Please telex us your design and consultancy fees and any other condition that might apply.'

Jones added in the press release: 'The American efforts to buy and install the Australian-designed keel on an American yacht in time for the Cup finals appear to be in direct contravention of the NYYC's own 1980 resolution governing the America's Cup, which requires each competitor's boat to be designed by nationals of that country. Most significantly, it appears curious to us that the syndicate backing the leading yacht in the defenders' trials has tried to purchase our keel design while the NYYC and now the USYRU is attempting to have the design re-rated by incurring a penalty.'

Jones added that the Bond syndicate had kept all details of the boat secret, 'apart from divulging full details in strictest confidence to authorities such as the Measurement Committee, whom we trust implicitly. If the NYYC is in receipt of specific information it can only be through improper means and we have the right to know who passed it to them and under what conditions.'

Accompanying the press release was a copy of a letter Jones had sent three days earlier to Dr Beppe Croce, president of the International Yacht Racing Union protesting at the actions of the NYYC to 'circumvent the agreed upon rules of the America's Cup 1983 by asking the IYRU to reconsider the rating of Australia'.

The IYRU announced on August 18 that it would meet on August 30 to consider the USYRU's request that Australia II be re-rated. Before that however, the whole issue collapsed with the revelation by the British challenger Victory's syndicate on August 22 that it had been experimenting with winglets on Victory 83 with the approval of the IYRU's keelboat technical committee more than a year beforehand. The committee ruled that 'tip wings are permitted so long as the static draft is not exceeded'.

'Keelgate' took its next turn with the NYYC pursuing the Bond syndicate under the Cup condition that all competing yachts must be 'designed by nationals of the country for which they compete'. On August 24, alerted by newspaper reports in The Netherlands of the Dutch contribution to the Australia II keel research, Richard S. Latham, a member of the NYYC America's Cup committee and Johan Valentijn's uncle Will Valentijn, arrived at the NSMB and tried to persuade Dr Van Oossanen to sign a two-page affidavit they had prepared concerning the work that the NSMB and NLR Aerospace Laboratory did for Lexcen and the Australia II syndicate.

Van Oossanen refused to sign it, at the time saying in a telex to Warren Jones on August 25: 'This affidavit contained many incorrect statements which attempted to suggest that Ben Lexcen was not solely responsible for the design of Australia II.' In that telex, Van Oossanen also said that he had told Latham and Will Valentijn that the NSMB and NLR Aerospace Laboratory had 'acted solely pursuant to Mr Lexcen's directions at all times. 'I further informed Mr Latham that the computer support work provided by the NLR Aerospace Lab and tank-testing at NSMB for Mr Lexcen is similar to the computer support work and tank testing provided by the Delft University of Technology here to the designer of Liberty and Magic in 1981.'

[By then Johan Valentijn, the Dutch-born designer of Magic and Liberty, was a US citizen, married to an American and living in Newport.]

Dr Van Oossanen added in his telex to Jones: 'I find the New York Yacht Club's position and efforts in this matter deeply disturbing and offensive. I hope they will have the good sense to desist from further untrue charges attributing the design of Australia II to anyone other than Ben Lexcen.'

Warren Jones, with the telex from Dr Van Oossanen also released a copy of a letter from Victor Romagna, secretary of the NYYYC's America's Cup committee, dated June 11 in response to earlier correspondence by Jones: 'Officially your tank tests in the Netherlands Ship Model Basin are entirely within the rules if:

1: They were under the sole supervision of Australian nationals.

2: The designs were from the drawing board of Australian nationals.

3: Results are used in the design of that Australian challenger only.'

ON AUGUST 25: IYRU chief measurer Tony Watts confirmed to Tom Ehman of the US Yacht Racing Union that the interpretation given to the Victory syndicate in August 1982 also applied to the Australia II keel. Next day, New York Yacht Club Commodore Robert Stone and Commodore Robert McCullough, chairman of the America's Cup Committee, announced at a press conference in Newport that the question relating to the keels of Australia II and Victory '83 and their designs had been resolved.

The press release announcing this contained a reservation about the designer nationality issue. It said that having been put on notice by Dutch newspaper articles that the keel design was the product, if not the invention of Dutch experts, the club, as trustee under the America's Cup Deed of Gift, was obliged to investigate the matter, 'to be satisfied that the terms of the trust are fully complied with by all participants.

Australia II navigator Grant Simmer and Alan Bond / ROSS

'Having completed such investigation as we felt necessary and proper we have concluded that the evidence available to us to date is insufficient to press the matter further at this time. With these matters resolved we can now all focus on the match itself to be settled on the water and may the better yacht win.'

Lexcen, heavily restrained by Warren Jones from talking to reporters during the Keelgate saga, had a rare opportunity to score verbal points on the issue on August 30. When the Australia II crew returned early to the Newport dockyard from a Louis Vuitton finals race against Victory '83 aborted before the start through lack of wind, they found a set of crude wings being fitted to Freedom, pacemaker for Liberty. The wings, about 1.5m long and 0.75m wide, were made of plywood covered in fibreglass. They were curved on their upper surfaces and flat underneath.

Liberty's designer Johan Valentijn, who was supervising the rush three-hour job, said that Freedom would test the winged keel against Liberty's before Liberty's scheduled race against Courageous in the New York Yacht Club's defender trials the following day. Valentijn had just finished explaining to reporters that he was unsure whether the wings would make Freedom any faster but felt that this design departure should be explored, when Lexcen appeared on the scene, grinning from ear to ear.

'They are going to have an awful lot of trouble with the NYYC trying to get it measured,' he said. 'It will do little more than give the barnacles more space to grow on their boat; they have put a barnacle farm on their keel.

'It is completely whacko. They know nothing. Defender is putting on wings too, but under wraps (Defender, by then eliminated from the US defence trials, was then the warm-up boat for Courageous) The British showed me their wings and I could not figure out why they did not make them slower. But the wings on Freedom are big enough to slow you down like mad. It is hard to do those things.'

Lexcen then commented on Alan Bond's announcement the previous day that he would reveal the keel to the world on September 12, the day before the America's Cup. Lexcen and others in the Australia II team wanted to keep it hidden. 'If they see the keel is only made of lead, is not alive and does not glow, then the fright value is gone. But if you keep it hidden and beat them in an early race, they will call in the witch doctors.

'If we had not hidden it, they would have had one on their boats so fast ... this is America; they put rockets in the sky. We are just rolling around in the dirt, digging out iron to sell it to the Japs. They would have had a keel made of lead just the same as ours if we had shown it to them and now it is a great psychological weapon.'

A crowd developed around Freedom at the Newport Offshore dockyard as workmen swiftly finished installing the wings. Lexcen finally borrowed a pencil and walked across to join Valentijn at the keel. He signed his name on Freedom's wings and added: '51 out of 100 for effort'.

Three days after that ebullient moment, the stress of the keel dispute, on top of the self-imposed workload in refining Australia II, felled Lexcen, who was already on medication for high blood pressure. He was suffering from a viral cold, became dizzy and on September 2 was admitted to Newport hospital after his blood pressure sky-rocketed. The hospital discharged him on September 7 after he passed tests that included a stress test.

His Australia II team mates saw the hospital stay as a welcome break; an opportunity for the highly-charged Benny to relax. Typically, he was able to extract a laugh from it. I encountered him in the street a day or two after he left hospital. 'See that guy over there?' he said. 'He's the doctor who put me into hospital. He hooked the cardiograph machine up to me back to front and it went crazy,' he said. 'I would not trust him with my pet dog.'

Keelgate was by no means over. On September 5, the day Australia

II officially became the America's Cup challenger, beating Victory '83 in the concluding race of the Louis Vuitton Cup for a 4-1 winning score in the final and a record of 48 wins and six losses in the whole 54-race series, the NYYC America's Cup committee, renewed the attack. Richard Latham in a press release attached a copy of a letter he had written to Dr M.W.C. Oosterveld, head of the research and development division and Dr Van Oossanen's superior at the NSMB, demanding a public retraction of the statements made Dr Van Oossanen in the August 25 telex to Warren Jones.

It referred to the August 24 meeting that he and Will Valentijn had had with Dr Van Oossanen, at which Dr Oosterveld had been present. Latham said he had presented Dr Van Oossanen with a draft of an affidavit seeking confirmation of the roles of the NLR Aerospace Lab and NSMB in the design of Australia II. The letter said: 'I can understand how Dr Van Oossanen, out of friendship for Ben Lexcen and in light of the repeated emphasis Dr Van Oossanen placed on the expectations of further consulting work with Mr Alan Bond, might decline to put his name to statements, the content and substance of which he admitted were true.

'I cannot, however, comprehend how you, Dr Van Oossanen's superior and as a senior official of NSMB, an institution with an international reputation, would suppress the truth and at the same time seek to conceal the important contributions by NSMB and NLR to the conception of the keel design – and indeed the entire hull – of Australia II.'

Twenty years later, when I visited Dr Van Oossanen at Wageningen to hear his side of the story during the campaign to have Lexcen inducted into the America's Cup Hall of Fame, he admitted that when Latham presented him with the affidavit and asked, 'Is it factual, he had replied: 'I can't really answer that. I am as much Australian as any Australian, having lived in Australia for 15 years. I have an Australian passport. I wouldn't be Australian in the context of the America's Cup rule. Nevertheless, I feel I'm Australian; I feel part of this team. I don't want to hurt them in any way.

'Before he left, Latham said, 'Alright, off the record, is the affidavit true or not true?' and I said, 'It's totally true.' So, he knew exactly what happened but there was no evidence whatsoever.'

The New York Yacht Club inexplicably missed the opportunity to see Australia II's keel by being present at the international measurement committee's measurement of Australia II in June, before she began her winning sweep. It sent Johan Valentijn along to a check measurement of the America's Cup challenger at the Cove Haven Marina at Barrington, 15 miles from Newport, on September 10, by measurement committee members Mark Vinbury (USA) and Jack Savage (Australia).

The measurements to be checked were mainly waterline length and draft; measurements that could have been made with the keel still shrouded. However, the Australia II team decided to allow Valentijn to see the keel to accelerate or defuse any potential protest situation. Although the NYYC had said the legality of the keel was no longer under challenge for this America's Cup, under the conditions of the match, it was still open to Liberty as a competitor to file a technical measurement protest under the racing rules.

The check measurement became a circus. Because of the tide's timing the yacht could only be hauled out at midnight. Coincidentally some weeks before, that night had been chosen by the Cove Haven Marina for a party for its customers – mainly the Victory '83 crew – and its yard workers and sub-contractors. So, when Australia II arrived to be hauled out and measured, she was greeted by a crowd of more than 200 partygoers, plus journalists and television crews. Also joining them were Liberty's skipper Dennis Conner, tactician/navigator Halsley Herreshoff and Valentijn who drove up in a pickup truck with an American flag draped over the bonnet.

The crowd began singing 'God Bless America' as the hoist lifted Australia II out of the water with the keel the crowd had hoped to see shrouded in plastic. The song petered out after one verse. The travel lift carried Australia II minus mast, which had been earlier plucked out by crane, into a huge shed and the doors slammed shut. Inside, Vinbury and Savage went about their task of re-checking the main measurements under the scrutiny of Valentijn, with Lexcen and Warren Jones among the Australia II onlookers, locked up in the shed for about three hours.

Later that day, Valentijn told me that the session had been amicable. 'I had a great time. I was with Ben, like the good old days you know. We have always got along very well together. We chatted about our boats in an amicable way. I told him what I had tried to do with Magic and said why I thought he had succeeded and I didn't succeed.'

Valentijn said he had reported to the NYYC's America's Cup committee that he didn't see anything basically wrong with Australia II. 'I told them it was very interesting. That's all I can say.' He said he thought the keel was a 'very clever piece of equipment'.

He said that Australia II was probably the most radical Twelve Metre he had seen. 'It is very different, very innovative. It took a lot of balls to build that boat. I was gutsy with Magic but I they were as gutsy to build Australia II.'

Commenting on the psychological warfare, Valentijn said: 'I have to give Warren Jones a real lot of credit. He has done the greatest job anyone has ever done in this whole America's Cup business. He is the only one who has approached it professionally. He is a good businessman and he also knows how to use the press to his advantage.

'He has done a fantastic job this summer. He is running this whole America's Cup show in Newport. Alan Bond and Ben should be very thankful they have him around. I wouldn't mind having him on my side the next time.'

ON SEPTEMBER 11, three days before the start of the America's Cup, the NYYC America's Cup committee fired its last shot in the Keelgate battle. Its chairman Bob McCullough presented Alan Bond with a 'Certificate of Compliance', along the lines of the affidavit Richard Latham had asked Dr Van Oossanen to sign.

The first of its ten points read: 'Australia II was designed solely and exclusively by Ben Lexcen, a national of Australia, and no 'foreign consultants' and no 'foreign designer – however he is designated' assisted in the design of Australia II's keel, hull, rig or sails.'

And the second was: 'All tank tests leading to the design of Australia II, conducted in the Netherlands Ship Model Basin, were under the sole supervision of Australian nationals in accordance with the letter of June 11, 1982 from the America's Cup Committee to the Australia II Syndicate, a copy of which is attached hereto.'

But besides these basic conditions, the Certificate of Compliance looked much more restrictive. It asked the signatories to state that the Australia II syndicate and Ben Lexcen had not contracted with or retained the NSMB or NLR Aerospace Laboratory perform consulting or research services to assist in the design of Australia II or contribute any invention or design concepts which led to or were incorporated in the design of the keel, hull and/or rig of Australia II.

It also asked the signatories to acknowledge that:
• No proprietary or confidential computer programs were developed for or made available to Ben Lexcen in developing by computer the design of the keel, hull and/or rig of Australia II.

- The engineering, design details of the taper and scarf splice and the fittings on the US-made spars of Australia II were Ben Lexcen's.
- Computers and other electronic equipment aboard Australia II were either designed and manufactured in Australia or were standard shelf items.

The document was to be signed by Commodore Peter Dalziell on behalf of Royal Perth Yacht Club, Alan Bond, Warren Jones and Ben Lexcen. When Bond and Jones declined to sign, McCullough went to Bill Fesq, representing the Challenger of Record Royal Sydney Yacht Squadron, showed him the Certificate of Compliance, told him of Bond's refusal to sign it and reportedly demanded that he 'find another challenger'.

Fesq refused and next day the Cup committee met to decide whether to proceed with a match between Liberty and Australia II or cancel the America's Cup races. Michael Levitt and Barbara Lloyd in their book Upset reported that four members of the committee wanted to continue with the match and five wanted to pull out. Those who backed down were concerned about the outcry that would follow from the public and the seven challenging syndicates who had been campaigning in Newport all summer. So, the Cup went ahead.

The NYYC America's Cup Committee comprised: Commodore Robert W. McCullough (chairman), Commodore Henry H. Anderson Jr, Robert N. Bavier Jr, Briggs S. Cunningham, Stanley Livingston Jr, James Michael, Vice Commodore Emil Mosbacher Jr, Richard S. Latham, Victor Romagna (secretary).

ON SEPTEMBER 12, the day before the scheduled first race, the flag officers of the NYYC decided to accept general representations by the Australians of compliance with the provision in the Conditions Governing the Races for the America's Cup 1983, which read: 'Yachts shall comply in every respect with the requirements regarding construction, sails and equipment contained in the Deed of Gift and the Interpretive Resolutions applying to national origin of design and construction.'

On the nationality issue, the three-page, ten-point Certificate of Compliance, was far removed from the Cup's original Deed of Gift, drawn up by donor George L.Schuyler and the NYYC and filed in the Supreme Court of the State of New York in 1857, which simply said that the challenging yacht must be 'constructed in the country to which the challenging club belongs'. Since then, the Deed had been amended twice, in 1882 and 1887 and had three sets of Interpretive Resolutions with the 1958 change interpreting 'constructed' as meaning 'designed and built ...' and 'designed' as meaning, 'the designers of the yacht's hull, rig and sails shall be nationals of that country...'

FROM UPSET: 'DID Ben Lexcen design Australia II or the Dutch? Lexcen's response indicated that it was a group effort: 'They (the staff at NSMB) were just doing what I told them. Sometimes they would tell me things back. How the hell can they stop them from telling you things.' It's like in a jury, 'Well disregard that remark'

Warren Jones; always on top through the keel controversy / ROSS

... You can't disregard that remark. If someone says, 'I think this could be a good idea, you can't say, 'Well I didn't hear that.'

'The situation at the tank puts you almost under conditions that would contravene the spirit of the bloody ruling of the New York Yacht Club but as far as I am concerned, if you can use the tank, then you can talk to the people at the tank. The only time they brought it up was after the boat was good but they never would have bought it up if the boat had been a turkey.'

It would have been hard not to have gathered ideas in such a creative environment. And yacht designing, sails and equipment by 1983 was becoming multinational. By 1987, America's Cup challengers were being designed by teams, including scientists, drawn from beyond national borders. In 1996, Bill Koch's winning America Cubed team, within a

US$65 million budget, brought the Cup to a new high level of technology with a design team that included two scientists, Dr Jerry Milgram and Dr Heiner Meldner in charge of the design program, traditional yacht designers Doug Peterson, John Reichel and Jim Pugh and a whole raft of technical experts.

Bruce Stannard in 'Ben Lexcen, the man, the keel and the Cup' quotes Ben: 'I went to Wageningen like a dry sponge. I soaked up an incredible amount of knowledge there. I learned all sorts of esoteric stuff, like dolphins and what makes them swim fast. It all went into my head and allowed me to see things very clearly and formulate new ideas. I used their brains, I used their knowledge and their experience. But that's not cheating as the New York Yacht Club claimed. For me it was like going to university and sucking all that knowledge out of the professors. The process of design is so complex. It's hard to say were one person's ideas start and another's takes over.'

# 14

# THE AMERICA'S CUP WIN

YEARS ON, THE 1983 AMERICA'S Cup win is still like a dream; a sequence of incredible events over 14 days that ended in a heart-stopping way; Australia II coming from behind on the running leg to gain a narrow lead at the last mark and taking the seventh-race decider from the defender Liberty to win 4-3. Ben Lexcen's radical design Australia II through the challenger elimination series showed a superiority in speed and tacking ability that had the New York Yacht Club defenders worried. Equally important was the calm, professional approach of her crew and close-knit organisation directed by executive director Warren Jones built on the experiences of previous challenges. Alan Bond, whose presence had sometimes been disruptive in the earlier challenges, this time took a backward step and let Jones handle the administration of the team and negotiations with the increasingly fearful New York Yacht Club.

The winged keel was not just an appendage that could be discarded if it did not work, but part of a total design concept that allowed Lexcen to produce a relatively lightweight hull with lots of sail area. Australia II, at about 50,000lb displacement was the lightest Twelve in Newport; around 3000lb lighter than Liberty. The winged keel overcame the stability that had prevented previous attempts to design lightweight Twelves from being successful. It concentrated weight low down with each of the wings, made of lead, weighing about 3500lb. The wings also made the relatively short and shallow keel more efficient by reducing the tip vortex drag-producing flow from the bottom of the keel. They streamlined the water flow along the keel instead of allowing it to slide off the bottom.

The little keel and the absence of the large bustle usual in the conventional Twelves to fair in the hull aft of their large keels, besides reducing wetted surface area drag, allowed the hull to spin through a tack or a gybe much more quickly than conventional Twelves. This useful weapon in pre-start manoeuvring was eventually negated by tactics devised by Liberty's afterguard: Skipper Dennis Conner, tactician Tom Whidden and navigator Halsey Herreshoff. But quick tacking remained an extremely effective weapon in Australia II's armament. Her skipper, John Bertrand, could spin the boat from one tack to another and

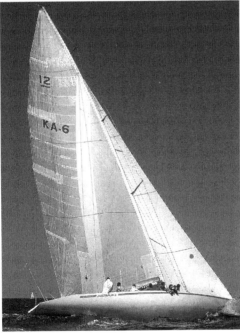

1983 Australia II / ROSS

almost immediately pick up the new course without having to pull away that degree or two, to build speed before coming up to course on the new tack and Australia II was also quicker to accelerate out of the tack. Any time Liberty engaged her in a tacking duel, Australia II could respond comfortably and gain distance on Liberty with each tack.

Australia II's tacking ability influenced Liberty's upwind tactics. Instead of adopting the conventional match-racing tactics of continually tacking to every tack of a trailing opponent, Liberty would keep hunting out wind shifts while trying to maintain a covering role to avoid being pulled tacking duel exchanges by Australia II. In some races, this approach worked for Liberty; most notably in race four where Conner and Whidden exploited every wind shift to win after leading all the way from winning the start. In some other races, it was Liberty's undoing; especially in race six where Liberty, lifting on port, did not take that one more tack back onto starboard needed to cover Australia II which sailed into an even bigger port tack lift and gust which shot her into 2min 29sec lead at the first mark.

Australia II's sails equalled those of Liberty and some of them, notably the spinnakers, were more effective. They were developed with input from many sources – Bertrand and his tactician Hugh Treharne were sailmakers; designer and off-boat adviser Lexcen was a former sailmaker – through a program co-ordinated by Tom Schnackenberg, a New Zealand-born Australian resident who dropped out of studies towards a degree in nuclear physics to go sail making.

Schnackenberg and his five-man team of sailmakers refined a new construction method, using vertical instead of horizontal panels, to fully utilise the low-stretch characteristics of the newest Kevlar/Mylar cloth laminates to produce lightweight, beautifully-shaped sails. They went to shallower, closer-winded sail shapes, equally important as the efficiency of Lexcen's keel in giving Australia II its ability to point very high to windward.

Although John Bertrand did not always look quite as masterful as Dennis Conner in the match-racing game, he was certainly good enough and probably more of an inspiration to his crew. Bertrand recovered from the crushing blows to his confidence of equipment breakdowns in the first two races that cost Australia II at least one win. Down 1-3, he ground his way back to the 4-3 win with inspiring mental and physical toughness. He and his crew just treated each race as another one to be won. Their one-day-at-a-time approach did not allow the intrusion of any thought that they were battling 132 years of history as well as a rival yacht. They were supported by an equally close-knit and experienced onshore organisation that, besides putting the crew each day into a perfectly-prepared racing vehicle, sheltered them from outside pressures.

The long controversy over the legality Australia II's winged keel was coolly handled by Australia II's executive director Warren Jones. He repelled every attack by the Liberty syndicate through the New York Yacht Club as it came. Standing securely behind the International Yacht Racing Rules and the America's Cup Conditions, he confidently defended his yacht. And by adroit use of the media, he turned public opinion throughout the USA and those parts of the world remotely interested in sailing, against the New York Yacht Club. He disclosed that the Liberty syndicate had firstly tried to buy the keel design from the Netherlands Ship Model Basin and then, when that failed, tried to secure admissions that the Dutch technicians, not Lexcen, had been principally responsible for the design.

Bond left the day-by-day administration of the challenge to Jones, who was a director of Bond Corporation and its trouble shooter; a role eminently suiting him to directing his third America's Cup challenge for Bond. Earlier in the campaign John Longley, as project manager, was responsible for the daily administration under fairly distant supervision from Jones. But in Newport Longley, a big and strong veteran of all the previous Bond challenges, was to sail in the crew. So, Jones picked up the daily administrative duties for the party of 34 people in the crew and its support group, helped by his secretary Alison Baker and public relations officer Lesleigh Green.

The executive group included Lexcen, a former sailmaker who also designed sails for the boat and acted as an off-boat adviser together with Sir James Hardy who, besides being a director of the challenge, was relief helmsman for Bertrand. John Fitzhardinge, a trustee of the challenge syndicate, was race controller – he organised informal training races and was syndicate observer on race committee vessels controlling the official racing. Laurie Hayden was sports psychologist and Glenn Read, from Mark Bethwaite's championship-winning Soling crew, headed the syndicate's computer programs and electronics. Mike Fletcher transferred from Challenge 12 as coach.

The sailing group of 12, plus Longley, comprised in the tactical decision-making back end of the boat: John Bertrand skipper/helmsman; Hugh Treharne, tactician; Grant Simmer, navigator and Colin Beashel, mainsheet trimmer. The three winch grinders were Peter Costello, who had sailed on Australia in the 1980 challenge, Will Baillieu and Brian Richardson, both former world champion and Olympic rowers. The three headsail trimmers, Rob Brown, Ken Judge, Skip Lissiman, mast man Phil Smidmore and the bow man Scott McAllister, had all sailed in previous Bond challenge crews. Longley and Costello alternated in the 'sewer' under the decks forward, packing and preparing headsails and spinnakers. When McAllister had to withdraw from the crew after breaking his arm while trying to free a jammed main halyard during the challenger elimination series Damian Fewster from Challenge 12 became bowman on Australia II for the challenger final and the America's Cup.

Manning the well-equipped purpose-built tender Black Swan were Phil Judge (skipper) and Newton Roberts. Ken Beashel, the Sydney boatbuilder and former 18-footer and 16ft skiff champion, headed a hard-working and highly-competent maintenance team with Steve Harrison, Mark Reid and Dave Wallace. They operated from two containers; one fully equipped as a workshop and the other housing spare gear.

The racing spanned a record 14 days including four lay days (two called by each boat), two days when the wind was too light or unreliable to start a race and one day when the time limit ran out with Australia a long way ahead, as well as the seven races.

RACE 1 (SEPTEMBER 14): Wind at start 045 degrees, speed 18 knots; at finish, 050 degrees, 18 knots. The start was evenly contested. Australia II, after slowing Liberty with a sharp luff on the final approach, hit the line three seconds ahead but with Liberty, very close to windward. Within a minute Australia II, sailing very high, was exhausting disturbed air into Liberty's sails and Liberty tacked away. When they first crossed tacks Australia II was ahead. Liberty gained a slight lead at the next cross then Australia II, on inside of a slight lift on starboard tack, was able to cross ahead of Liberty, tack onto port and carry her all the way to the lay line to the first mark before tacking away first on starboard for the mark and rounding 8sec ahead.

On the first reach of the triangle-windward return-windward-finish course, Australia II held off Liberty and gybed around the wing mark 10sec ahead. But on the second reach, Liberty sharpened up and with her longer waterline (by about 18in) and setting a flat staysail inside her flat-cut reaching spinnaker, took a 16sec lead at the leeward mark.

From top: Race one start, 1983 America's Cup.
Australia II leads around the first
mark race one / ROSS

Conner and Whidden exploited the wind shifts intelligently and Liberty rounded the second windward mark 28sec ahead. Australia II, sailing deeper and faster became almost overlapped with Liberty on the run and was almost overlapped when, on the final gybe to the mark, one of the five under-deck pulleys in the steering system broke, sending Australia II into a partial broach. Bertrand got the boat back down to course with the trim tab but the steering breakdown contributed to a messy spinnaker drop and mark-rounding with headsail and mainsail not sheeted on for half a minute. Although Australia II rounded the mark 35sec behind she lost more than another minute while the steering was restored with a block and tackle jury rig. Liberty won by 1min 10sec.

RACE 2 (SEPTEMBER 15): Wind at start 030 degrees, 17 knots; at finish, 055 degrees, 10-13 knots. The race was really decided in Liberty's favour six minutes before the start when Australia II had another equipment failure. Australia II, while gybing, was hit by a gust of 24 knots and broke the upper one of the two specially-hardened steel lugs used to hold the medium-air mainsail headboard to its carriage. The headboard swung down, pivoting around the lower lug and then the whole head of the sail tore along the lower edge of the headboard. The sail was left hanging 12 inches from the top of the mast, secured only by a one-inch diameter piece of Kevlar line sewn through the headboard and the top of the leech as reinforcing. This left the boom drooping onto the deck.

Race one, Liberty powers over Australia II second reach / ROSS

After debating whether to retire, the crew decided to continue, achieving some tension on the leech of the mainsail by raking the mast as far forward as it would go with the hydraulic adjustment on the forestay. The boat was, as a result, badly out of balance all race with Bertrand having to contend with two or three degrees of lee helm when the wind fell light on the second and third windward legs. Australia II tacked off onto port soon after the start and after a short port tack was first into a heading shift. She tacked, crossed ahead of Liberty and survived a tacking duel – 14 tacks in four minutes – to hold a 45sec lead at the windward mark.

Colin Beashel spent 18 minutes up the mast on the two reaching legs securing the head of the main to the masthead carriage with lashing passed through a hole he punched with a spike through the head of the sail. Liberty closed to within 31sec at the gybe mark and 21sec at the leeward mark. The repair could do no more than ensure the sail did not completely fall; it was not possible to achieve any more leech tension so the sail, which had got by in the slightly over-powering breeze of the first beat, was completely inefficient for the second windward leg with the breeze down to eight knots and going patchy with wind shifts of 30 to 35 degrees. Bertrand and tactician Treharne, reasoning they could not now win the race with routine match-racing covering tactics

195

Australia II ahead race two, despite broken headboard / ROSS

against a faster Liberty, chose instead to chase puffs and work the shifts. Within half a mile of the windward mark, though she still appeared to be in less breeze, Liberty picked up a good starboard tack lift which enabled her to get back into the middle of the course and cross Australia II by a comfortable five or six boat lengths. She rounded the mark 48sec ahead, Australia gained to 31sec on the run and on the final beat, with the breeze down to five knots at times and her mainsail completely inefficient, was beaten by 1min 33sec.

[Liberty 2-0]

RACE 3 (SEPTEMBER 17) was abandoned when the five-hour 15min time limit ran out with Australia II leading 1.5n miles from the finish. She had led around every mark after winning the start in a 10-knot breeze, held a margin of 1min 15sec at the first mark, 1min 58sec at the end of the two reaching legs, 1min 46sec at the second windward mark, 5min 57sec at the end of the run. Australia II sailed the perfect race but was deprived of a certain win by prolonged calm patches on the last three legs of the course. Finally, with all hope of finishing within the time limit gone, the breeze piped in again, in a perverse way, at a steady seven knots.

Race 3 resail (September 18) wind at start 225 degrees, seven knots; at finish 230 degrees 10 knots: Liberty was passive in the pre-start manoeuvres, reluctant to tangle with Australia II's superior manoeuvrability now well proven. Conner worked hard to start at the committee boat end, free to tack and stand on to the right-hand side of the course which the expected first wind shift would favour. Bertrand worked on different meteorological information which suggested the left-hand side of the course would be favoured early in the race as the new south-west breeze filled in before it followed the traditional swing to the right.

Conner tacked onto port in the last minute and headed right at the gun. Australia II soon after tacked to follow. Both yachts stood for a 22m speed test with Australia II sailing two degrees higher, steadily climbing out to windward. When Liberty finally tacked onto starboard, Australia II crossed five boat lengths ahead. Liberty threw in seven tacks, including a false tack, to try and break Australia II's covering shadow. But Australia II, faster through a tack and faster in accelerating from it, kept increasing her lead. She rounded the windward mark 1min 14sec ahead.

Liberty gained to within 52sec on the first reaching leg and with a slight wind shift making the second reach shier, made effective use of her 2.8oz flat cut Mylar staysail inside the spinnaker to gain another 10sec on the second reach. But Australia's 42sec advantage at the leeward mark gave Australia II a nice covering edge out of the mark. Liberty tried everything on the second windward beat: straight-line speed sailing alternating with quick-tacking exchanges. But Australia II stretched out to a 1min 15sec lead at the end of the second beat, went away to 2min 47sec down the run and kept going away on the beat to the finish to win by 3min 14sec.

[Liberty 2-1]

RACE 4 (SEPTEMBER 20) Wind at start 235, 10 knots; at finish 235 degrees, 15 knots. Liberty won the start by six seconds after what John Bertrand said, 'was an error of judgement on my part'. Australia II was gaining on the first windward leg until Liberty, on port tack with Australia II following on her windward quarter, dug into the major header of the race, tacked for a major gain and rounded the first mark 36sec ahead. Liberty gained 12sec on the first reaching leg and the margin remained

Running, a weakness early in the campaign,
became Australia II's strength / ROSS

48sec at the leeward mark.

Up the second beat Liberty, sporting a good-looking medium-air mainsail for the first time in the series had equal speed and height with Australia II. Conner and Whidden avoided being drawn into tacking duels and made the best use of the wind shifts as they came, playing leading boat tactics as if they were in a fleet race with covering a slightly secondary consideration. This left Australia II no option, with the breeze remaining reasonably steady in direction, but to follow suit and stay in touch with Liberty, which led around the second windward mark by 46sec. Australia II was again faster on the run, pulling back the margin to 35sec. But with the wind freshening to 15 knots on the final beat Liberty, again exploiting first use of the shifts, gained slightly to win by 43sec.

[Liberty 3-1]

RACE 5 (SEPTEMBER 21) Wind at start 190 degrees, 18 knots; at finish 185 degrees, 16 knots. Liberty broke her port jumper strut while she was warming up against Freedom one hour before the start. Liberty first sought permission from the race committee to have a spare strut flown out from the shore by helicopter. When this request was refused, it sent its fastest support boat the 11 miles back to Castle Hill, at the mouth of Narraganset Bay, where it picked up the spare set of jumpers from an inflatable runabout. Meantime pit-man Tom Rich and bow man Scott Vogel were hauled up the mast to dismantle the damaged strut. The replacement was passed to Liberty and the repair completed just two minutes before the 10-minute warning signal to the start. Vogel and Rich returned to the deck exhausted and bruised after more than 50 minutes of being thrown around and against the mast, set swaying by a bumpy seaway. Then, as members of the three-man foredeck crew, they had to wrestle with the task of hoisting a headsail, now urgent with the yachts about to engage in pre-start manoeuvres. In their haste, the luff tape securing the sail to the forestay was not properly fed into its groove and tore away. That left Liberty easy prey to Australia II while the damaged sail was hauled off the deck and another headsail hoisted. Fortunately for Liberty, she could split Australia II off her tail by diving around behind a 350ft Coast Guard vessel.

Liberty, despite these difficulties, was still well positioned on her final approach to the line, level with Australia II and to windward on starboard tack, poised to tack off for the right-hand side of the course where Conner again felt the first favourable wind shift would be found. Bertrand was intent on starting to the left of Conner, closest to the America's Cup buoy end of the line. But for the second race in a row, Bertrand misjudged his approach, Australia II slid across the line early with very little speed, which made the return slow and Australia II eventually started 37sec late. With both boats on port, Australia II quickly began to gain. Then three or four minutes after the start, Liberty's port jumper strut again broke – the repair had not been completely effective because the hydraulic cylinder had been damaged and the rod remained fully extended, sticking too far out of the tubular strut, which was why it collapsed in the first place.

Without full tension on the port jumper stay, the top of Liberty's mast kinked out to leeward on port tack. The boat was still sailing fast, but lower on port tack. Fifteen minutes after the start, Australia II tacked away from Liberty and stood on starboard towards the middle of the course. Conner, reasoning that Liberty's best option in her crippled condition was to gain distance on the wind shifts, continued on port, feeling that the wind direction would clock to the right, so Liberty continued on port for another five minutes before tacking onto starboard.

Australia II, which had split a long way to the left, sailed into a five-degree header, tacked and when the two first met, 27 minutes after the start, Australia II was dead even with Liberty and tacked back onto starboard under Liberty's lee bow. After they exchanged ten quick tacks in five minutes, Australia II was ahead, gaining a few metres with every tack, pushing Liberty to the right and protecting the left. Australia II rounded the first mark 23sec ahead, held the same margin at the wing mark, lost slightly on the second reach to round the leeward mark 18sec ahead.

Race six, Liberty took an early lead after winning the start / SOEHATA

Pointing higher and accelerating from tacks faster, Australia II increased her lead on the second windward beat to 1min 11sec. Hoisting a bigger spinnaker, that was efficient in the fresh breeze, Liberty closed to 52sec on the run. But Australia had enough lead to cover Liberty up the final windward beat to win by 1min 47sec.

[Liberty 3-2]

Australia II peels to the half-ounce runner; one of the successful spinnakers developed in Newport / SOEHATA

RACE 6 (SEPTEMBER 22). Wind at start 340 degrees, 12 knots; wind at finish, 260-290 degrees, 16-19 knots. Bertrand again misjudged the start. After shaking up to it on starboard tack early, he had to gybe Australia II and circle back to port to cross behind Liberty and start seven seconds later. Liberty tacked onto port, gained slightly by being on the inside of a lift and crossed Australia II when she came back on starboard. Australia II, four minutes after the start stood on a long starboard tack towards the left-hand side of the course, expecting the north-north west breeze to back through the west and freshen. After 14 minutes Australia II tacked onto port. Liberty tacked dead in front, ahead by two boat lengths. Australia II tacked back onto starboard on a header. Liberty, confident in working the port tack lift, did not go back to cover. Australia II, after sailing another 100 metres, tacked back onto port on Liberty's quarter.

Liberty sailed into a lull and headed down while Australia II, in a fresher patch of breeze, lifted out steadily and dramatically. After ten minutes, Liberty sailed into a slight header, tacked onto starboard and struggled back towards Australia II. Australia II crossed ahead and slammed over onto starboard, hard on Liberty's air, forcing her to tack back onto port. Australia II sailed on into a gust that contained a huge port tack lift. She tacked onto it and lifted almost straight to the mark with Liberty still plodding along in much less air now a long way dead to leeward.

Benny anxious; Tom Schnackenberg relaxed / SOEHATA

With the wind down to five knots at the mark, Australia II rounded with a luxurious lead of 2min 29sec. The wind freshened back in to 12 knots on the first reach, turned into a very shy one by the wind shift. Australia II rounded the wing mark with a perfectly executed gybe-peel to a running spinnaker for the third leg, now a dead run. Much livelier on the light run, she held a big 3min 46sec lead at the leeward mark.

The course was changed to 295 degrees for the second windward beat but the wind continued to march to the south-west and freshen. Australia II's covering pattern, ensuring that she always stayed between the left-hand of the course and Liberty, put her into another 30-degree backing swing in the wind which allowed her to lay the last third of the work to the mark on port tack and denying Liberty any chance of recovery. Conner tried one last desperate move. With Australia II coming away from the mark under spinnaker on starboard gybe, with the running leg turned into a beam reach by the shift, Conner, still beating to the mark, pulled away on starboard tack and tried to 'nail' Australia II by, at worst, fouling her or making it awkward for Australia II to keep clear as she had to as windward boat. Australia II altered course dramatically to avoid any chance of a protest by Liberty and cleared Liberty's bow by two boat lengths.

Australia II held a 3min 22sec lead at the second windward mark, was 4min 8sec ahead at the leeward mark. Liberty's crew work – poor spinnaker set, ultra conservative takedown – reflected a lowering of morale in the face of a huge deficit. Australia II covered easily on the windward work to the finish, with the breeze now very fresh, to win by 3min 25sec.

[Australia II 3-Liberty 3]

Australia II gybes around last mark, race seven,
with a spinnaker float-off / SOEHATA

SEPTEMBER 23 WAS a lay day, called by Australia II to rest the crew and give the boat a thorough check before the deciding seventh race. Harold Cudmore, the Irish match-racing expert, who had dropped out from the British Victory '83 challenger crew after a disagreement with syndicate head Peter de Savary, steered Challenge 12 in practice starts with Australia II during the afternoon, helping Bertrand sort out his starting problems.

Liberty during the lay day re-trimmed internal ballast and added sail area to try and match Australia II's light air speed. About 920lb of lead was removed and the lighter displacement figure allowed an increase of about 23sq ft in sail area taken up by extending the foretriangle J measurement from 24.5ft to 25ft. Liberty had used this device during the defender trials, to the annoyance of rival syndicates who did not know about it until the end of that series. The boat had three different measurement certificates, for heavy-air, medium-air and light-air sailing modes, allowing variation of the displacement to sail-area ratios for the different wind strengths.

September 24: After the second attempt to start deciding race seven, the race committee postponed racing for the day because they considered the conditions – wildly shifting and fading breeze off the land from the north west – to be unfair for both yachts. Liberty after the postponement called a lay day for September 25. The Australia II crew

Last beat race seven / PAUL DARLING

spent the afternoon of September 25 practising starts and sailing short races against Challenge 12, helmed alternately by Harold Cudmore and Bruno Trouble, skipper of France 3. Liberty's crew after going through the tedious process of preparing their yacht for another ballast change and re-measurement decided not to change with the late-afternoon weather forecast suggesting a light-air race the following day.

RACE 7 (SEPTEMBER 26) Wind at start 205 degrees, 8 knots; at finish, 200 degrees, 8 knots. The yacht race of the century started cautiously. Neither crew wanted to be involved in any protest situation. Both yachts alternatively drove on then stalled in the last two minutes with Liberty to windward, positioned to go off on her favoured right-hand side of the course and Australia II happy sail to the left. Liberty tacked away and started on port, officially 8sec ahead at the gun, but Australia II, continuing on starboard, crossed the line with better speed than Liberty which had to dip back at a sharp angle after her tack to stay behind the line before the gun.

Liberty was the first to tack, onto starboard, heading back towards the centre of the course, three minutes after the start. Australia II tacked onto port five minutes after the start and a minute later Liberty tacked away onto port, a concession that she was unable to cross Australia II. The wind was shifting up to 20 degrees and 30 degrees up that first leg, Bertrand said later, with major changes in velocity as well. Twenty minutes after the start Liberty tacked onto starboard and Australia II crossed on port, three or four boat lengths ahead.

At the second cross, three minutes later, Australia was still ahead by two boat lengths and kept going on port tack for four minutes before tacking onto starboard, allowing Liberty to split a long way to the left. The Australia II afterguard believed they did not have enough wind pressure to quickly tack and cover Liberty and that the next shift would come from the right. The shift instead was a header from the left with a slight freshening in the breeze, which knocked Australia II down towards Liberty's line. When the yachts next

Race seven winning tow home / PAUL DARLING
Warren Jones embarrasses Ben Lexcen,
last race press conference / ROSS

met, eight minutes after second crossing, with Liberty on port hitching back towards Australia II on starboard, they were dead even. Liberty tacked on Australia II's lee bow, forcing Australia II onto port to clear her air. The shifts continued to favour the left. Liberty came back on port, crossed ahead of Australia II and tacked, still closest to the now looming port-tack lay line to the mark. Liberty tacked back to port and Australia II on starboard, now a long way from being able to cross Liberty, tacked under her onto port. After a short starboard tack, Liberty rounded the mark 29 seconds ahead.

The more powerful Liberty gained on the first reach, turned into a shy spinnaker carry by a backing shift of ten degrees and was 45secs ahead at the wing mark. The shift turned the second reaching leg into a squarer spinnaker angle, suiting the fast-running Australia II. She closed to 23secs behind Liberty at the leeward mark.

Liberty dictated the tactics on the early stages of the second windward beat, covering Australia II, which flopped onto starboard soon

Australia II after finish of last race / ROSS

after rounding the mark and then tacking onto port when Australia did and immediately gaining by being on the inside of a long and slow port tack lift. After the exchange of four tacks that followed, with Liberty looking at times to be a minute and a-half ahead, Australia II sailed into a header that lifted her on the port tack approach to the mark to round 57secs behind.

Liberty, soon after rounding the mark, gybed onto port and sailed towards the centre of the course to get away from the interference to wind and water from the heavy concentration of spectator boats near the mark. Australia II kept going on starboard gybe, along the spectator fleet line but into fresher breeze which had been apparent on that side of the course during both of the upwind legs.

After two minutes on port gybe, Liberty gybed back onto starboard to keep in touch with Australia II but she looked slower and in less air. After five minutes, with Australia II still on starboard gybe obviously continuing to improve, Liberty gybed away and tried to work wind shifts towards the middle of the course to keep her lead.

Australia II, able to sail deeper angles with better speed than Liberty under a more stable looking spinnaker and mainsail, exploited two shifts down the run, gybing only five times to Liberty's nine and she dragged Liberty into sailing lower, squarer angles. She easily escaped the attempts of the more cumbersome Liberty to blanket air from her sails three-quarters of the way down the run. Australia II cut across to the inside of the course to ensure gaining an overlap at the mark, laid back precisely on starboard and with the perfect float-off spinnaker drop gybed around the mark 21sec ahead.

On the beat to the finish, Australia II held off a determined attack by Liberty which engaged each yacht in 45 tacks – Liberty continually splitting tacks to try and keep clear wind and force Australia II into error; Australia II carefully maintaining her cover. Conner twice tried the false tack – dummying to tack his yacht and then falling back to his original heading - while Australia II was left hung-up, head to wind, more committed to completing her tack.

Two-thirds of the way up the leg, Australia II looked to be losing ground, being drawn too closely into Liberty's game. Realising this, the Australia II afterguard stretched out the covering tacks a little

Australia II and Challenge 12 show underbody differences / ROSS

more and gained. Eventually Australia II close-covered Liberty almost into the spectator fleet beyond the starboard tack lay line before tacking over to lay the finish.

She won by 41secs.

ON THE TOW into port, syndicate head Alan Bond and Lexcen, who had climbed aboard Australia II, decided to unveil the keel when Australia II was lifted out of the water at her berth in Newport Harbour. While most observers had a rough idea of how it would look, a big crowd gathered on the dock and some in inflatable dinghies were stroking it. Lexcen said at the press conference which followed: 'The keel has about 500 people hanging off it at the moment. When we lifted the boat tonight there were just heaps of them, hanging off it like leeches when you walk through a swamp. They are going to start a new religion.'

Asked if Australia II's boat speed had been equal Liberty, Lexcen said: 'The whole boat speed was equal to Liberty's but were pushing big Dennis Conner. I was worried about Dennis Conner. Dennis saved the Cup last time and deserves a lot of credit for trying to save it this time.'

To the next question: 'Even though you had the faster boat, he could somehow pull it off?

Lexcen answered: 'He's a tricky little devil.'

Asked 'On the first two upwind legs Liberty seemed able to hold you but on the third leg, you seemed to do much better.'

Lexcen answered: 'Well I guess our guys were learning on the first couple of upwind beats; I don't know, I was asleep on the second upwind leg.'

Questioner: 'Bullshit,'

Lexcen: 'It's true.'

Asked what the win meant to him, Lexcen replied: 'A damn bloody big relief; it's a 12-year dream come true.'

Would Australia have won without the winged keel?

'Maybe, maybe not; who knows. Challenge 12 in today's conditions used to beat Australia II pretty regularly and I think with similar tuning and similar crew you would find Challenge 12 to be just as fast. When we conceived Australia II and I was convinced it was faster than a regular boat, I was pushing to do two radical boats the same. But Alan (Bond) in his wisdom said, 'No, we should build a regular boat and a radical boat.'

Lexcen added that when the first Victorian syndicate behind the conventional Challenge 12 got into financial trouble and a new group took over it gave the Bond syndicate the opportunity to proceed with the radical boat. 'I was always confident to build the radical boat; I would have preferred to build two radical boats. Afterwards I was happy we had done Challenge because it pointed out to us the failings in our boat that we had to try hard to correct.'

Worship as the keel is unveiled / SOEHATA

Ben later gave this description of the keel to Bob Ross, for publication in Australian Sailing magazine:

*ANY KEEL SERVES to develop lift to help the sailing qualities of the boat and as a package for the ballast. In the Twelve Metre rule there is no measurement of stability so the lower the centre of gravity, the better the boat. The upside-down inverted profile shape of the keel and the wings lower the centre of gravity. There is no bulb, as everyone believed, the keel just gets a little* thicker at the bottom in accordance with its chord and protruding from it for about half its length on the bottom, it has wings about 2.5m long, 60cm wide, made of lead – very thick and very heavy with each wing weighing about 3500 lb. The keel weighed a total 40,000 lb. Total displacement

Benny with the America's Cup plate / SOEHATA

of the boat was 53,000 lb. Because of the low centre of gravity, we could have a lighter-displacement boat that also had more stability for heavy weather. So, we had a light-weather and heavy-weather boat all in one.

The wings also increase the effective span of the keel, giving less leeway and less drag for a reduced keel size. Australia II's lift-drag ratio is 45 per cent better than that of an ordinary keel. When a yacht with a conventional keel is heeled, draft is reduced where ours gains a tiny bit of draft from the wings as the yacht heels up to 12 degrees. At 12 degrees, we have the same draft as a conventional boat when the conventional boat is upright.

The keel also has very good hydrodynamic qualities running because at 25 degrees chord the sweep angle is zero where a conventional keel has a slope of 30 to 40 per cent. A sloping (back) keel breaks the boundary layer on the leading edge and you end up with a turbulent flow on the keel when running. With our keel, we could expect to have a laminar flow condition over the whole keel, especially when running. Airplanes that fly below 500 mph, like the wartime Spitfires and Mustangs and light planes like Cessnas, have zero sweep. The chord width, a lot shorter fore and aft than a conventional keel's, means the boat must be more manoeuvrable, you don't have to twist a lot of keel through the water.

The winglets stop the cross flow at the bottom of the keel. Angled downwards 20 degrees, they each set up a vortex revolving clockwise. The two vortices clash together, meeting with the side of one vortex

Benny with the keel / SOEHATA

*going up, hitting the side of the other vortex going down, to negate each
other. So, there is no revolving wake behind the keel and the keel span
is made effective right to its tip. With a regular keel, the bottom 46cm
is ineffective. The winglets are cambered on both sides and sloped down
at the front and up at the back to most efficiently meet the water flow*

*which runs uphill at the bottom of the keel.*

*The trim tab attached to the trailing edge of the keel, weighing 700lb, was also more effective because it operated above the bottom of the keel sealed off by the winglets. It worked in turbulence-free water and was carefully faired into the keel with a plastic membrane either side. Up to seven degrees of trim tab was used – which is a lot – to effectively increase the curvature of the keel and so gain more lift from it upwind.*

*In summary: the keel allowed me to design a light boat with stability to go well in a strong breeze, with a cut-away profile aft as well as forward and a small keel all adding up to improved manoeuvrability.*

# 15

# LOSING THE CUP
# AND THE END

'WHEN I WIN THE CUP, I will be free,' Ben Lexcen once told his friend Carl Ryves. That feeling, perhaps, told against his preparation for defending the America's Cup in Fremantle, in 1987. The campaign was by no means as precisely focussed throughout the Bond syndicate as it had been for the 1983 challenge and Lexcen at times seemed to have lost interest.

Lexcen formed a new design team after the 1983 win, based in Sydney and involved in varied projects to fill in the down time on the America's Cup defence program.

Firstly, in 1983, he signed on Peter Lowe, who had worked for Peter Cole and Associates as a draftsman for a number of years and who at the time was finishing the design of an oil rig supply vessel when the company went bust.

Yacht designer friend Bob Dummett, knowing Lowe would soon be out of a job, suggested he approach Ben Lexcen. 'I talked to my wife about it and rang up Ben,' said Lowe. 'Yvonne answered the 'phone and she was very defensive because at that time, he was being pestered by everyone under the sun.

'I have been told Ben is looking for a draftsman.'

'She said, 'He will talk to you.' She put him on and he said, come around to the house in Clontarf and bring a few of your drawings.' We went downstairs to his office and chatted for a while. He rolled out my drawings and said, 'Shit, ink! I will give you three months trial.''

The first boat Lowe worked on with Ben, from offices in Dee Why, was a One Tonner, Apollo VI, built by David Warren for Alan Bond, to race on the Swan River and contest the 1985 Admiral's Cup trials in Melbourne with Colin Beashel as skipper. She won the first race of the trials; proved very fast in light air, was not remarkable in heavy air and finished seventh in a closely-fought eight-race series. 'Bondy's only requirement was that the deck didn't leak,' said Lowe.

They then became more heavily involved in the Twelve Metre program, moved into offices into a new complex of boating businesses in Careening Cove and gradually built up a design team of three or four people.

Through 1984, Lowe worked with Lexcen on an America's Cup Twelve Metre design for a South Australian syndicate, to be involved as a partner in a two-boat tuning/training program similar to that between Australia II and Challenge 12 in 1983. The design was tank tested at the Netherlands Ship Model Basin where the Australia II design was tested.

In April 1984 a Perth-based syndicate, headed by Kevin Parry, confirmed its intention to build a contender with Iain Murray as skipper and co-designer with John Swarbrick, on a $4 million budget. It booked in for research at the NMSB in May.

Syd Fischer, whose Alan Payne-designed Advance was a total disappointment in a campaign for the America's Cup in 1983, also decided to build a challenger, to a design by Peter Cole.

Lexcen in May 1984 visited the Netherlands Ship Model Basin and watched the testing of two new models representing refinements of his Australia II design as part of the design program for the Twelve for the South Australian syndicate. On the basis of those tests, Lexcen designed a third model and was to return to Holland at the end of June to test it.

However, he collapsed and became critically ill while he was in Prince Henry's hospital in Sydney having some routine tests for an old neck injury which had been bothering him. Apparently allergic to the

Australia II re-launching ceremony,
Fremantle, August 1984

testing dye, he collapsed while in a private room at the hospital and when found was blue in the face and not breathing.

He was revived, but his blood pressure, a long-time problem for him, shot up to an alarming degree and he was kept in the hospital's intensive care unit for a week, then sent home to rest.

Australia II went back in the water in August 1984 for tuning and training and though November and December for the SA and WA syndicates' eight-week evaluation program. Lexcen did not lock up the design of Australia III until that program was completed. Australia II was to be sailed as strongly as the new boat and if Australia III and Australia II in the 1986 world championship proved to be completely off the pace against some other radical new boat, a crash building program would produce Australia IV.

Eclipse 30, Ben's own JOG boat, 1986 / ROSS

Through three series of five races in Adelaide in May 1985, Australia II consistently defeated South Australia. The lack of experience among the South Australians told against them, especially in starts. South Australia was skippered by Fred Neill. Gordon Lucas and then Colin Beashel, on his return from match racing contests, steered Australia II. Each boat sailed with their regular crews.

South Australia did

win the first race of the first series over the full America's Cup course by 58sec but Australia II won the remaining four by margins varying from 20sec to 3min.

South Australia went back to builder Steve Ward to have her keel shifted forward 5cm; she had been sailing with 544kg of lead trimming ballast stowed inside ahead of the mast. Ward had already started to build Australia III.

As the second anniversary of the America's Cup win approached in September 1985 and with it the launching of Australia III, a born-again Ben Lexcen was zestfully attacking a massive-looking workload, still indulging his passion for fast-and-fancy Italian sports cars, planning his own sailing campaigns, throwing out ideas and opinions (many of them outrageous) and generally being his old self.

Being with him in his busy Sydney design office for an interview in July, 1985, was like re-opening a 13-year-old door to the time when he had designed a pair of successful ocean racers, Ginkgo and Apollo that had just broken the Sparkman & Stephens domination of offshore design in Australia and was doing the preliminary work for his first Twelve Metre, the adventurous but unsuccessful Southern Cross.

THE YEARS BETWEEN held for Ben a heavy measure of frustration and some failure, shadowed always by the struggle to hold the creative flood within the safe limits of sometimes indifferent health. Winning the America's Cup, the greatest success of any yacht designer's career, while wiping away the disappointments of those in-between years, brought new pressures. After being emotionally and physically drained by the event itself, Ben had to drag himself through the glad-handing, public speaking, being-a-hero, round and then face the realities of defending the America's Cup.

But now, with confidence in the Twelves he had designed for the defence and with seven other design projects under way, he seemed contentedly busy.

How could he do it all? Ben waved at his staff of three – Peter Lowe, Kalevi Savolainen, Brad English – and says: 'These guys do it' and adds that the computer has been a big help too. He has, however, been working hard and re-activated his office at home where he works nights. 'Work here consists mainly of answering the 'phone,' he said.

The Lexcen team's current projects (building or still in design stage) were: 18ft skiff, BOC Challenge around-the-world single-hander, 5.5 Metre, Six

Metre AmAus challenger, Admiral's Cupper, Junior Offshore Group 'maxi' and opulent motor yachts of the 23m to 43m overall variety.

Ben was about to move his design office to bigger premises in the new Careening Cove complex, which that had replaced the Dickensian stack of timber and corrugated iron that formerly housed the Hood sail loft and various riggers, painters and yacht engineers. He was about to add a youngster to his staff.

He explained that he needed to keep staff to handle the Twelve Metre work and must have other projects to keep them occupied in the down time on the Twelves.

He was happy at the way the Bond syndicate's campaign was going and that had a great to do with his (relative) peace of mind of the moment. 'I now think we can win the Cup,' he said. 'I was really worried a couple of months back. I think some of those American syndicates are starting to show a few cracks although there will be one that will not crack and become the challenger.

'But our whole thing is going perfectly to plan. We haven't really had a hiccup in it, although we have had some annoyances, Beasho (Colin Beashel) and Hughie (Treharne) have done well in match racing overseas and that problem we had is going away as we give more guys exposure to international match racing.'

What about Australia III? 'Australia III is as well as can be expected. It is going to be born on the right day – come out of the shed and be launched on September 27 (second anniversary of the Cup win in Australian time) and it is a full-on super boat. It is a continuation of what we have learned from building the South Australian boat.'

Although the underbody would be concealed at launching, Australia III would have a winged keel and would not be greatly different to South Australia. 'Australia III will definitely be better than the other two; it will have a bit of an edge,' he said. 'The South Australian boat is marginally better than Australia II when you put the right crews on it.

'It is the only boat I know that can out-tack Australia II and actually pass it. Sometimes, in a straight line, Australia II is faster, sometimes South Australia just takes off, but only when it is hooked up right.

'The South Australians know their sails were a bit wrong and their crew is not right and they are doing something about it. This summer they will be pretty good; they'll get some people, put their act together and be hard to beat. At least, they will be formidable opponents.'

Lexcen said there would be another Twelve after that and he was obviously excited about it. 'I have some ideas which, I think, are going to make it a breakthrough again; just as big a breakthrough as Australia II was.'

America' Cup Defence 1987 Ltd (Bond syndicate) was building its own masts in Perth to Lexcen designs. He was excited about that, too, reckoning as many man hours had gone into designing the mast as into the boat. After voicing his views of the industry's mast makers in terms too strong to print, Ben said they were tied down by business expediency, not to 'making a wonderful thing.'

He added: 'In the Twelves, we have got to make a wonderful thing so we are making the whole mast ourselves and it is going to be like a moon rocket. We have set up a factory in WA and got in people who are aircraft fitters to do it properly. Last America's Cup we were locked into Stearn masts and all those failures we had were legacies of that. We had to spend thousands of hours making them safe and we had to compromise on some things.'

Lexcen said the mast fittings had been engineered to be maintenance free. All of them had been tested to destruction.

IN JULY 1985 Lloyd's Ships, builder of quality large aluminium motor yachts at Bulimba on the Brisbane River, announced that Lexcen had joined them with his first commission, a 93-footer. Lloyds had 12 motor yachts under construction and with the extension of the Federal Government's ship-building bounty to include exports had begun marketing strongly overseas.

Ben said that he had been interested in luxury motor yachts for some time, had been impressed by Lloyds since on a visit to the Netherlands Ship Model Basin, while models of Alan Bond's 1974 America's Cup challenger Southern Cross had been testing there, he had watched powerboat and ship testing – 95 per cent of the facility's testing was applied to propulsion efficiencies.

Large aluminium power cruiser under construction at Lloyds Ships, Bulimba, on the Brisbane River, July 1985

Ben's 40ft powerboat built by David Warren Yachts / PETER LOWE

Was he really that keen, as he had sounded during the announcement, about the 'gin palaces'?

'Oh yes. I view that as exciting. For a start, it helps make this a viable business. It helps pay for the 5.5 and those fun things we do.'

Ben spilled out a folio of sketches he had been 'scribbling at home in the evenings'. One, predictably, had a Ferrari as well as helicopter on the back deck (Ben's own Ferrari was in pieces at the time, but he still loved them).

'I have come into this not knowing a lot about it so what I have been doing is just let my mind wander, sketching things like this. They are wanderings and I have got hundreds of them. I have tried to get the feel of these things. I'll know when I am right. I know I can do a better one than John Bannenberg (famous Australian-born motor-yacht designer living in London) and then I'll just set up the business so we can have a couple of guys just ram right into it.'

Ben produced drawings of an interior that a client wanted in a bigger boat. The observation deck included such 'essentials' as a movie theatre, bar and grand piano while above that, the owner had the privacy of a top deck with Jacuzzi spa, sauna, Nautilus gym, circular bed/lounge.

'It's fun to design such boats. I have ridden on lots of them and know

Australia III / ROSS

the mentality of the people. You walk down the back here and it all opens up and becomes a little private beach with plastic palm trees that pop up and a sandy beach for swimming and water skiing. They go for that stuff, these guys.

'That's all exciting. It's a little bit commercial compared to the yachts but it is creative. It's not like building a tug or a ferry; it's an exciting living thing. The client has to be satisfied with this just as much as if it were a racing yacht – probably more so. It's all mechanical, has to work nicely and look good.'

Peter Lowe, who in 1987, six months before Lexcen died, became a 50-50 partner with Lexcen in Lexcen Lowe Yacht Design, says he enjoyed working with Ben. 'I got on very well with him because obviously he was very, very clever although he went off on some funny tangents at times. It took me a while to realise that if I didn't think something was that good, I would say so and usually get a bit of a bad reaction. And then he would walk in next morning and say, 'I thought about what you said; you are right.'

Lowe saw himself as being complementary to Lexcen. 'I am a detail man and Ben at that time wasn't. I would take the rough drawings off him, play around on the computer and sort them out; fill in the gaps while Ben became inspired by something new.

'I was quite happy working with him. I worked a lot of hours because I was enjoying what I was doing; what I got paid didn't cover the hours I put in.'

Australia III leads the reaching pack, Twelve Metre worlds, January 1986 / SOEHATA

Australia III was similar in concept but slightly bigger all round than Australia II with more volume in the ends and a bigger bustle ahead of the rudder. Australia IV was a bigger boat again, aimed towards excellence in a higher wind range.

With Colin Beashel at the helm, Australia III won the Twelve Metre World championship at Fremantle, contested by a 14-boat fleet of America's Cup contenders, in January 1986, with conservative but consistently correct tactics plus a minimum of breakdowns and crew foul-ups.

She won with a race to spare, scoring 4-2-1-6-1-1-dnc for 22.7 points, from New Zealand KZ5 (Chris Dickson), the second of three fibreglass Twelves designed by a committee of Bruce Farr, Laurie Davidson and Ron Holland, with a scoreline of 1-3-5-3-3-7-3, 32.8. Third was America II (John Kolius), 2-7-4-2-6-4-2, 36.7; fourth Australia II (Gordon Lucas), 3-4-7-1-5-2-6, 38.4; fifth French Kiss (Mark Pajot), 7-1-6-7-2-6-1, 39.4.

Any one of these five had speed enough to win the regatta but in ten days of untypically light breezes with big (15-20 degree) wind shifts, fortunes were as mixed as the weather.

Local knowledge was not much use. The famous 'Fremantle Doctor' strong south-west sea breeze was at home firmly only for the seventh heat at 18-25 knots. Three of the races were sailed in westerly or WNW breezes and the winds for two races were quite light: 6-8 knots for race four; 8-14 knots for race six.

Notable absentees were the Kookabur-ras, who chose not to race and Dennis Con-ner's Stars & Stripes syndicate, which had shrewdly based itself in Honolulu for two years to test full-size five boats and crews in the steady trade winds of Hawaii in preparation for the 12-30 knot sou'westers expected off Fremantle during the America's Cup regatta.

Australia III and Australia II,
Fremantle, 1986 / ROSS

Through September 1986, Bond and Kevin Parry's Taskforce syndi-cates strove to tune and assess their newest boats, Australia IV and Kooka-burra III. Both designs were pitched towards excellence in heavy air but the weather was alternating between very light and very windy; too windy at times to test anything except the strength of boats and crews.

Australia IV, startlingly faster than Australia III upwind in heavy winds was depressingly slow, to about the same degree, running in light air.

Although Kookaburra III had shown great upwind speed in strong winds and the ability to pace Kookaburra II in the light, she was on her way back to the builder's shed for modification in mid-September. The original boat in the Taskforce line-up, Kookaburra I, was given 10cm more freeboard and a complete re-furbish and could still be one of the two boats Taskforce would field in the defender eliminations.

The Taskforce syndicate finished Series A of the defender elimi-nations in the strong position of having Kookaburra III on top of the points table and Kookaburra II in third place only a point behind the Bond syndicate's best yacht Australia IV and only two points behind the leader. The two yachts were very even in speed though Iain Murray believes Kookaburra III was faster downwind in very windy conditions, seemed faster to tack, or at least come out on a higher line and accelerate more quickly after a tack, than the other defender candidates.

Colin Beashel and his very experienced tactician Hugh Treharne on Australia IV quickly realised this and broke out of tacking duels to chase advantageous wind shifts, certainly in their matches with Kookaburra III.

Australia IV had equal straight-line speed with the Kookas in all conditions. Lexcen felt the tacking advantage of the Kookaburras was due to the close-quarters nature of the racing they had been having in their preparation for the regatta than anything in the hull design. He added a very fine canard fin, running between the leading-edge tip of Australia IV's heavily-bulbed wing keel and the hull before Series B. And the combination of a faster Australia IV and the more confident crew allowed them to keep splitting the Kookaburras at the head of the points table.

The Bond syndicate and especially designer Lexcen, were scratching their heads over the poor performance of Australia III. The yacht that just eight months earlier had won the World Twelve Metre fleet racing championship just looked off the pace, able to beat only South Australia and Sydney Steak 'n Kidney.

Straight after the series the Bond syndicate's wily executive director Warren Jones was asked if there was a lot left in tuning and development for Australia III, which had been in the water 14 months. 'Common sense dictates no, said Jones. 'What we are observing is a step forward with the latest Twelve Metres and I think Sir James Hardy (sailing director of the South Australian syndicate will agree – South Australia and Australia III are sister ships.

'The Kookaburras and Australia IV are subsequent designs that have evolved as people have got used to the conditions out here. It is fairly obvious that these three boats are a step forward and it going to be very difficult for the slightly older Twelve Metres to match them.'

At the end of Series B, in which a win counted two points, the scoreboard was Kookaburra III 29, Australia IV 20, Kookaburra II 19, Australia III 12, South Australia 8, Steak 'n' Kidney 0.

The whole defender eliminations format was thrown into confusion by the Bond syndicate's withdrawal of Australia III at the end of Series B, the retirement of South Australia (John Savage) after only four races in Series C and the dramatic but late improvement of Sydney Steak 'n Kidney (Fred Neill).

The Bond syndicate, in retiring Australia III, said it had been surpassed by the next generation of Twelves like Australia IV and the two Kookaburras and it wanted to concentrate all its resources on Australia IV.

Earlier, the syndicate had insisted Australia III was still a fine all-rounder, doing her job of covering the lower end of the wind range where Australia IV was vulnerable. The implication was that skipper Gordon Lucas with his tactician Carl Ryves and navigator Nigel Abbott were making mistakes, but Lucas did not have the confidence in the boat and so did not sail well.

Start Australia IV and Kookaburra III, 1987 defender trials / ROSS

Kookaburra III came out of series D (semi-finals) as points leader on 83 from Australia IV 77, Kookaburra II 70 and Steak 'n' Kidney 24, eliminated three races from the end for not having enough points to have a chance to go onto the final (as required by the Notice of Regatta).

Phil Thompson, who helmed South Australia in the earlier Round Robins, steered Steak 'n' Kidney in Series D. The boat went out on a high note with an all-the-way win over Kookaburra III (Iain Murray) by 39sec in a 17-20 knot sou'wester that gusted to 30 towards the end of the race. Fischer, who funded Steak 'n' Kidney campaign almost totally with his own money, made her available as a pace boat for Australia IV for the finals.

Kookaburra II (Peter Gilmour) scored five wins and three losses in Series D while Kookaburra III and Australia IV each won four and lost four. The racing was extremely close between these three.

The finals were never as close as the semis with Kookaburra III gaining an upwind edge with a keel change in the break between the series to dominate Australia IV 5-0. The addition of Peter Gilmour was a good move. His aggression, quick reactions, sense of timing and sheer unpredictability won him two of the four starts, and an even start in another after he blew the first start of the final with a collision. His presence took a lot of the pressure off Murray who sailed the four races with much more confidence

Colin Beashel proved to be a cool and capable helmsman and with the 1983 veterans, tactician Hugh Treharne and navigator Grant Simmer, formed an afterguard that often out foxed the Kookaburras. In the end, however, they were devastated by a faster boat.

So, the Bond team had to watch while Dennis Conner, sailing an even faster boat, firstly beat New Zealand 4-1 in the challenger elimination final then beat Kookaburra III in the America's Cup match 4-0.

The Taskforce syndicate's research and development program, a big part of a budget that eventually blew out to $22 million-$25 million, which included tests of keels and wings in the Aeronautical Research Laboratory's Melbourne wind tunnel, was outstripped by that of Conner's Sail America Foundation.

Conner, stung by the edge in technology the Australians had with Australia II in her 1983 win, believed the Cup in 1987 would be won by a dramatically faster boat, not by a good match-racing boat and match-racing skills.

Supporting Conner's three designers – Britton Chance Junior, Bruce Nelson and Dave Pederick – were teams of researchers in computer design and tank testing drawn from the aviation, aerospace, defence and ship-building industries.

With a roster of five yachts, beginning with the 1983 defender Liberty and the Spirit of America 1983 defence candidate, both re-built and three new yachts – Stars & Stripes '85, Stars & Stripes '86, Stars & Stripes '87 – the design ideas were tested full scale off Hawaii, chosen by Conner because its 18-25 knot trade winds offered year-round approximation of the conditions to be expected off Fremantle in the latter stages of the challenger eliminations and the Cup match.

The program resulted in a yacht that was two-tenths of a knot faster upwind than Kookaburra III and in its own way just as much a design advance as the Australia II of 1983.

All of the match-racing skills Iain Murray and his Kookaburra III crew had developed through the tight racing in of the defender eliminations against Australia IV and Kookaburra II were of no use against this speed edge which Conner and his team used to play wind shifts and almost ignore the opposition. Conner said: 'It's a difficult problem when you are up against a boat like Stars & Stripes that won't play the match-racing game. When we won't tack and we won't cover, it's pretty hard for them to be aggressive and exploit the fact they do tack better and manoeuvre better.'

Ben Lexcen, in an interview with British yachting writer Barry Pickthall, reflected on the defeat of Australia IV: 'If there is to be any blame for Australia IV's failure to win through to the 1987 Cup final, then it falls on the Bond group as a whole including the designer.

'We stupidly changed the boat right at the start when it was a rocket

Kookaburra III and Australia IV, dead even at a windward mark / ROSS

ship in heavy weather and we paid for it all summer. We took 2000 lb of ballast out of the boat and bent the stern up to shorten the waterline length

'All summer we were chasing weather helm. Australia II had too much in strong conditions, so I designed Australia IV with a large package of ballast forward and a fin keel aft in an effort to get lateral plane aft and improve the balance of the boat.

'Everyone kept telling me that the boat needed more weight in the helm so I thought I had over-cooked it and added a canard forward of the keel. In fact, the problem was the exact opposite – Australia IV had too much weather helm and after we moved the mast forward six inches during the lay day in the final series, the boat was transformed.'

Contrary to reports at the time, the only other change made to Australia IV was the re-fairing of her wing tips – not a change of keel – and according to her designer, this did not have the detrimental effect on the boat's performance that others have asserted.

'After Australia II's victory, I helped draft the rules covering winged keels and said they should be the width of the boat, but when they wrote the rule they set the limit to minimum beam. I thought they had written it as I suggested and after designing the wings to maximum beam found that they were four inches too long. The wings were shaped like those of a Spitfire and after cutting the tips off the profile they became more like those of a Typhoon.

'The only problem was that they were a bit thick, so I said to the blokes between races, 'why don't we trim the wings back into a proper double ellipse and narrow the chord section by shaping some twist into the tips.' All told, we didn't cut more than a side-plate of lead away and then poured it into an empty bolt hole so we didn't lose any weight either.

'If anything, she was faster in the last series than before but the Task-force team raised their game even higher. In retrospect, I think that the Kookaburra hull lines are better than AIV but our keels, especially the one that we never had time to fit, which has exceedingly low centre of gravity, is better than the one on Kookaburra, which is really just an Australia II type with wide wings.

'The Kookaburra crew beat us because their boat was faster. What they did was run a continuous research program while ours went in jerks. We were always counter-punching rather than making things happen – reacting to a changing situation rather than making the situation, which was the way we won the Cup.'

Carl Ryves, Lexcen's close friend and sailing associate, who was tactician for Gordon Lucas on Australia III through the challenger eliminations, with the hindsight of several years, said: 'Australia III won the 1986 worlds against 16 other boats; the worst thing we could have done because it made the camp a bit complacent, but we never beat the Kookaburras. The few times we raced them, they were always faster than us but no-one would admit they were faster. They said, 'They got a better start or their tactics were better.'

'Australia III and South Australia were really good boats. Australia II was a 44ft waterline boat, Australia III was 44ft 6in on the waterline. I think the Kookaburras were always around 45ft 6in and Dennis Conner's big boat Stars & Stripes was a 47-footer.

'Then Australia IV was designed as a 46ft waterline boat and it was fine, except Australia III used to beat it all the time in winds under 12 knots so then they panicked and cut it down to about 45ft so when the wind did appear – when you cut the length down in a Twelve you have to take a few tonnes of lead ballast out as well – we lost our way a bit; got lost in the woods.

'Benny was never there to help us; he was there on the odd day but we needed him out on the boat, watching the others sailing. I don't believe he watched one race in the worlds. If he had been there and he had enough power to boss Warren Jones through Bondy, who would do whatever Benny wanted and then use his great talents to organise it.

'We had Jonesy making decisions which – I can remember pleading with him not to put a light keel on Australia III. They did it, wasted weeks and then cast a keel that was too light.

'We were supposed to have gained six inches of waterline with a big bulby keel. The builder said he made the pattern correctly, Benny said he designed it correctly, the foundry said they did the right thing, but whatever happened it came out to be two tonnes too light.

'They bolted it on anyway, made bigger sails for a boat that was already good in light air and we finished up with Australia III in the trials going back to its year before configuration.

'They said 'it's got to be alright. It's got the weight down lower so it will have the same stability and we can move the forestay out six inches, make the boom 18 inches longer.' And I was always sitting on Jonesy's table saying, 'don't do it, you're wrong.'

'The first day we went out with the new keel the boat was capsizing; the blokes in the leeward pit were under water. We'd wasted a month. We put the old keel back on, another two weeks and then went into the trials. We should have decided to re-cast the new keel.

'But we didn't have Benny there. He was over here (in Sydney) chucking his phone into the water.'

Ryves was referring to the incident when Ben, in his Careening Cove design office with Carl Ryves' sister Mary in attendance, was having a telephone conversation with Colin Beashel and Hugh Treharne in Fremantle. 'For whatever reason Benny was off with the pixies, you couldn't get any sense out of him, he was a tv star by then. Whatever they were telling him really upset him. He got more and more agitated and chucked the 'phone out of the window," said Ryves

'In the end he was the court jester to all those rich and famous guys he met; Bondy, the Agha Khan, Koshogi and that's when he changed from being the world's worst dresser to thinking he was pretty flash. He had a bit of money in those last five years so he used to buy the Gucci shoes and Cashmere jumpers. Yvonne gave me some of his Cashmere jumpers when he died and some of his shoes; which I figured he probably owed me because he had been pinching my clothes all his life.'

Peter Lowe saw the communication between the sailing team and the design team differently with constant changes called for Australia IV irritating to designer Lexcen and the reason he did not spend more time in Fremantle in the build-up to the Cup.

'Just as we were about to leave the office the 'phone would go – they hadn't thought about the two-hour time difference and they would say, 'We are thinking of re-trimming the boat; floating it up or floating it down and if we do this, what boom will we have to put on for it to rate as a Twelve Metre.'

The constant consideration of changes prompted Lowe to graph full-scale lines plans down to a millimetre of the models tested by the Netherlands Ship Model Basin so that changes to displacement and trim of the boat so that changes could be made quickly and accurately. Australia IV was the first Twelve they had that went in the water, had the mast put in, was measured and went sailing the same day. All the ones before that they had to play around with moving keels around, putting ballast in.

'Australia IV? They mucked it up,' said Lowe. 'If you look at any of the photos of the final trials, the back end is kinked up because we shortened the waterline at the bustle. In the light breezes they used to call Australia IV 'The Church' because it was so upright, where Conner's boat didn't go very well in the preliminaries at Fremantle but he stuck with it believing it would perform once they got to the decisive end of the final races, it would win.

'Where with Australia IV, we gave them what they asked for, which was a fresh air boat and then they changed it, slowly. Ben would leave

Benny with the Toy Fair Award he won a week before his death

the office and say, 'I am off to Perth for two weeks', or something like that and be back within week. The 'Gang of Four' (which Lexcen called certain key figures of the sailing team) would all have their opinion on what they should do so instead of staying over there for two weeks, he would come back. Everybody was an expert after the event.'

LEXCEN, WHO HAD been trading as Ben Lexcen Yacht Design Ltd and Peter Lowe formed Lexcen Lowe Yacht Design with offices based at Newport, one of Sydney's Northern Beaches suburbs, in September 1987. While they were joint 50 per cent owners, the business was managed by Lowe who reasoned that Lexcen did not want to be involved in the day-to-day running of a small design business.

After Lexcen died on May 1, 1988, Lowe changed the name to Peter Lowe Design, in accordance with the wishes of Lexcen's family. By then, the concentration was on large powerboats, because there was more money in that work than yachts, although the company did design 5.5s, Buizen sailing cruisers and some small cruiser-racers. Will Hardcastle joined Peter Lowe in the business about two months after Ben's death and was still there after 30 years.

12122637R00123

Printed in Great Britain
by Amazon